The Murder of Sarah Dormer and the Trial of Ann Heytrey

The Murder of Sarah Dormer and the Trial of Ann Heytrey

Uncovering the Truth

David John Eason

PEN & SWORD
TRUE CRIME

An imprint of
Pen & Sword Books Ltd
Yorkshire - Philadelphia

First published in Great Britain in 2024 by
Pen & Sword True Crime
An imprint of
Pen & Sword Books Ltd
Yorkshire - Philadelphia

ISBN 978 1 39903 264 3

A CIP catalogue record for this book is available from the British Library.

Typeset in INDIA by IMPEC eSolutions
Printed and bound in England by CPI (UK) Ltd.

Pen & Sword Books Ltd incorporates the Imprints of Pen & Sword Archaeology, Atlas, Aviation, Battleground, Discovery, Family History, History, Maritime, Military, Naval, Politics, Railways, Select, Transport, True Crime, Fiction, Frontline Books, Leo Cooper, Praetorian Press, Seaforth Publishing, Wharncliffe and White Owl.

For a complete list of Pen & Sword titles please contact

PEN & SWORD BOOKS LIMITED
47 Church Street, Barnsley, South Yorkshire, S70 2AS, England
E-mail: enquiries@pen-and-sword.co.uk
Website: www.pen-and-sword.co.uk

or

PEN AND SWORD BOOKS
1950 Lawrence Rd, Havertown, PA 19083, USA
E-mail: uspen-and-sword@casematepublishers.com
Website: www.penandswordbooks.com

FSC www.fsc.org
MIX
Paper | Supporting responsible forestry
FSC® C013604

Contents

Introduction

At 7.15 pm on Sunday, 29 August 1819, the village of Ashow in the heart of England, within the ancient forest of Arden in Warwickshire, was shook to its core by a young girl's scream at Dial House Farm. The scream would echo further afield when 13-year-old Mary Dormer walked into the bedroom of her mother – 59-year-old Mrs Sarah (Harris) Dormer – and found her slain body lying on her back on the floor, her heels pointing towards the door.

Sarah's 21-year-old maidservant, Ann Heytrey, was charged, arrested, and imprisoned at the County Gaol at Warwick, where she would remain until the following year, when she was tried at Warwick Assizes for Sarah's murder and found guilty. Ann was publicly hanged two days after – the last woman to be publicly executed at Warwick. And after being cut down, her lifeless body was taken to nearby Kenilworth, where she was dissected that evening in the back garden of the local surgeon.

That was over two centuries ago, and since then, many an author has written accounts of the events of that fateful evening at Dial House – all five recent titles conclude that Ann was guilty beyond all reasonable doubt.

My own family has roots in the Kenilworth area. My parents met in the late 1950s at Thickthorn, where my mother worked as a stable girl, and my father, a yard foreman, delivered horse feed. I grew up less than a mile from Dial House Farm. In 1970, my father took over as game keeper and head gardener at Thickthorn, and we spent four years there.

It all began one day at my local library while I was searching old newspapers on microfilm, and I came across a court report of a trail of a young girl at Warwick. For some reason I was struck and decided to research other females hanged at Warwick. I found eighteen between 1739 and 1820, Ann being the last. I have researched all eighteen, but it was Ann's which caught my soul, and I had to get to the truth. After reading other accounts, I had deep concerns over these stories, including factual inadequacies, as well as their conclusions. So began eight years of research that led to the first-ever reinvestigation into Sarah's seemingly motiveless murder. Little did I know then that I was about to open Pandora's box!

I had read the same court report, including all the witness statements, the local constable and surgeon's reports, and the trial transcript, but I also went further into what lay before – as I did, a different story emerged from out of the darkness which illuminated the truth.

It was honestly slightly confusing as to why I had discovered another story which until now had been hidden and never told. This is that story.

I never intended to try to solve this case, as after such a long time it would be almost impossible and extremely arrogant of me to believe that I could. I wanted to shine a light on the overwhelming doubt over the young woman's conviction by re-examining every word spoken – this, I believe I have achieved. It's not for me to judge at the end. I wish to leave that to you to decide, dear reader, as we go back in time and hopefully uncover what I believe is the truth of the events of that evening.

As we go back, please keep these words in mind, from the very foundation of English law and justice, the Magna Carta (Great Charter of Freedoms), signed by King John at Runnymede, near Windsor, in 1215: clause 40: 'To no one will we sell, to no one deny, or delay, right or justice'!

Chapter 1

Sarah (Harris) Dormer

Let's explore the known history of Sarah Harris, the unfortunate murder victim, and her family. Sarah Harris was born in early 1760 in the ancient Warwickshire village of Arrow, situated eight miles west of Stratford-upon-Avon. Arrow is close to the Worcestershire border, near to both Alcester and Evesham – and since the seventeenth century, the ancestral home of the Seymour-Conway family (Marquesses of Hertford) of Ragley Hall, the gates of which are within the village.

Later that year on Tuesday, 13 May, Sarah was baptized at the local twelfth-century parish church of Holy Trinity. She was the second eldest of the four children of Mr John Harris, local sheep farmer, and Mrs Mary (Brookes) Harris; she was sister of Elizabeth (baptized 1 December 1758), Mary (baptized 5 November 1761) and William (baptized 25 February 1763). Between the births of Mary and William, Sarah's parents were married at Holy Trinity on 23 August 1762. Tragically, her mother, died three years later and was buried locally on 9 February 1765.

It is still unclear why or when Sarah and her family left Arrow and moved the 23 miles north-east to the Warwickshire village of Cubbington. The village is situated 3 miles north-east of Leamington Spa. At the time, it was much larger than its Spa neighbour, mainly due to it sitting on the old sheep drovers' trail between England and Wales; as such, this may have been why Sarah's father moved the family.

On Monday, 6 July 1795, Sarah would be married to Joseph Dormer at St Mary's Parish Church by the curate, Thomas Warde, by 'special licence'.

Going back to the early nineteenth century, there were two marriage licences available to couples: the first was the 'common licence', which was unaffordable to the majority and would explain the rise in those children born out of wedlock, such as Sarah and her sisters Elizabeth and Mary. The second was the special licence that came into law during King Henry VIII's reign in the sixteenth century, which is slightly ironic!

To be able to obtain a special licence, the couple would have to write to the Archbishop of Canterbury, who, at the time, was the Reverend and Honourable John Moore. He would decree if they were able to marry; it was upon his decision if the licence would be granted at the cost of £2 to £3 plus 10 shillings tax, dependent on who you were and from where you came. However, there were three main advantages of a special marriage licence:

1. Because of the expense and trouble of obtaining the licence, it was a way of reconfirming one's wealth and standing within the local community.
2. Circumventing the requirement for the wedding banns to be published in the couples' local parishes would allow them to marry in secret, preventing any opposition to their union.
3. Circumventing the wedding banns allowed for a quick marriage, which was helpful if the 'blushing bride' was no longer blushing. This saved the embarrassment of trying to explain why your first born's birth predated your marriage date.

Joseph Dormer was the son of Ashow-born Joseph Dormer and Mary (Judd) Dormer, who were married at Holy Trinity Church, Coventry on Tuesday, 29 June 1751. They were a wealthy and highly respected local family with roots not only in Ashow but also in nearby Stoneleigh, Leek Wootton, Cubbington, Kenilworth, Leamington Spa, Warwick and in St Michael's, Coventry. Joseph was baptized on 20 January 1761 at the Ashow parish church, The Assumption of Our Lady.

As far as records show, Joseph had at least one sister six years his junior, Anna Maria Dormer, who was baptized on 29 January 1767 at The Assumption of Our Lady church. In 1788, Anna, now 22 years old, gave birth to a son, James Lee Dormer, who was baptized in

Ashow on 2 March with no father's name recorded. We will meet James again later in this story.

Joseph Dormer is recorded, on his and Sarah's marriage entry, as being still a resident of the parish of Ashow, whereas Sarah is recorded as a resident of Cubbington. So, any explanation on how they had first met would be pure speculation. However, Mr James Dormer is recorded as being a local farmer in Cubbington at the time, so it may well have been through him that they met!

After the couple's marriage, it is believed that Joseph and Sarah may have set up home in Cubbington or nearby Stoneleigh. If we go back to their marriage by special licence, there doesn't seem to have been any of Joseph's close family in attendance, as they relied on Sarah's father and Joseph's uncle, John Judd, to be their witnesses.

This brings into question the reason why they chose to be married in this way. Of the three main reasons, the first is doubtful; if they had wanted to reconfirm the family and their future standing, they would have married in Ashow.

For the third, if Sarah had been pregnant, the family likely would have not have been that concerned, as Joseph's younger sister had given birth to out of wedlock.

Which leaves us with the second: marrying in secret. This is more probable, as Joseph's banns weren't read out in Ashow, giving his family and the village no notification of his forthcoming marriage to Sarah. This is backed up by the fact that none of Joseph's close family members were witnesses at the wedding.

This would indicate that Joseph's marriage to Sarah, if known about, would have been most unwelcome to his family, though not so much to Sarah's, since her father was present. Joseph may have been betrothed to another, possibly a local Ashow girl, in which case, having met and fallen in love with Sarah would go against his family's wishes, so he married Sarah in secret. And as such, it is very doubtful that they would have initially set up home in Ashow.

Just seven months after Joseph and Sarah's marriage, their first child, Elizabeth, was born and blessed with her mother's looks. She was baptized at The Assumption of Our Lady church in Ashow on 16 February 1796. By now time may have healed some wounds, and Sarah might have been accepted into the fold once news of the impending arrival of the first grandchild was known; but maybe not by all, as she would still be seen and treated as an outsider by others in the village.

After Elizabeth came Joseph on 2 January 1798, James Harris on 31 December 1799, Harriet on 29 November 1801, Mary on 18 September 1806, and finally John on 20 April 1810, all of whom were baptized in Ashow. At the time of John's birth, Sarah was then aged 49.

No record can be found of where Joseph and Sarah were living then with six children. It must have been a substantial dwelling for a family of eight, but it wasn't their future home of Dial House. Up until 1812/1813, William and Hannah Adkins were the Stoneleigh Abbey, Leigh family's tenant farmers of Dial House Farm.

In 1812, William Adkins had drunk himself to death, leaving Hannah, who was in ill health, with their daughter to run the farm, which they couldn't manage. Around March 1814, Joseph and Sarah had taken over the tenancy of Dial House Farm, the largest farm on the Stoneleigh estate. Hannah left Dial House and moved into Ashow, where she died in early January 1824 aged 67, and was buried locally alongside her husband on 21 January.

The same month, the wider Dormer family greeted into the world twins, Louisa and James Dormer, the children of James and Elizabeth, who were baptized at St Michael's Church, Coventry on 21 March (Our Lady Day) 1814. The year before, on 18 November 1813, Sarah's eldest sister, Elizabeth, married Richard Sanders at Holy Trinity Church, Arrow. Sadly, she would never see her brother, William, marry Harriet Casey in Arrow on 9 October 1830.

Chapter 2

Ann Heytrey

In this chapter, we'll explore Ann's family history and background, so as to be more familiar with her status and to lend context to the events that follow. Ann Heytrey was born in 1798 in the South Warwickshire village of Charlecote, situated between Warwick and Stratford-upon-Avon. On Sunday, 28 October of that year, she was baptized at the parish church of St Leonard's. Ann was the youngest of four children and sister of William, Hannah and Thomas Heytrey, and the granddaughter of Reverend Thomas Rawbone. Her parents were William Heytrey, Charlecote-born labourer for the Lucy family of Charlecote (Park) Hall, and his wife, Wolfhampcote-born Mary (Rawbone) Heytrey.

Ann's mother, Mary, was born in 1753 in the stunning, and now sadly abandoned, ancient village of Wolfhampcote, Warwickshire, situated on the Northamptonshire border. Mary was baptized there by her father, the reverend, later that year on 21 October at St Peter's Church. Her sister, Sarah, was baptized at St Peter's Church on 23 November 1755, and her brother, John, on 6 December 1758.

Going back another generation, Reverend Thomas Rawbone was baptized at St Peter's Church on 6 December 1707, the eldest of the five children of Richard Rawbone and Judith (Wats) Rawbone: Elizabeth, 27 January 1712; Ann, 5 December 1714; Mary, 2 June-September 1720; and Jane, 24 October 1723.

The reverend's father was born locally in 1646, but wasn't baptized until 27 August 1742. He married Judith, who was also born locally, in 1685. Judith died on 25 October 1717, and Richard died at Wolfhampcote on 27 August 1742.

The Reverend Thomas married Ashbocking, Suffolk–born, Catherine Bushel on 27 March 1753. Catherine died in Wolfhampcote in January 1768, followed by Thomas on 5 April 1774.

By 1781, Ann's mother Mary was living in Sherbourne, where on Tuesday, 13 March 1781, she married William Heytrey at All Saints Parish Church, afterwards setting up home back in Charlecote. Two years later, their first child, William, was born and baptized at St Leonard's Parish Church on 26 July 1783, followed by Hannah on 31 July 1785, Thomas in 1797, and Ann in 1798.

In April 1785, when Mary was seven months pregnant with Hannah, tragedy struck for the first time, but sadly not the last, when young William died, aged 2. He was buried on 15 April in St Leonard's churchyard.

It was shortly after Ann's birth in 1798 that her mother became ill and remained so until her death in 1821; her care would fall upon Hannah, then aged 13.

In 1807, tragedy again struck the family when father William died suddenly at home and was buried at St Leonard's Churchyard on 29 March, leaving Mary, then aged 57, to bring up all three children, Hannah (22), Thomas (10) and Ann (9) without any financial support. This burden would fall heavily upon the shoulders of Thomas, now the man of the house.

It was the weight of this burden that would lead Thomas into a life of petty crime as he tried to support his family, which resulted in him being implicated in the murder of William Hiron in nearby Alveston on 4 November 1820. At age 24, the year after his sister Ann's execution, he would follow her onto the very same gallows at Warwick on Saturday, 14 April 1821, alongside three of his associates, Nathaniel Quiney (38), Samuel Sidney (28) and Henry Adams, (35).

After their executions, they were cut down and delivered for dissection under the direction of the high sheriff. Nathaniel Quiney was sent to the General Hospital in Birmingham, Henry Adams was dissected in Warwick, Samuel Sidney was sent to neighbouring Leamington Spa, and Thomas to Rugby.

As for Ann, her own young life (if you can call it a life) would follow the same pattern of so many other young girls and women back then from a lowly background.

Their futures were chained and would lie solely in the service of others. They would be worked to the bone for long hours with little pay, but they were fed, clothed and given a roof over their heads in exchange. And so it was for Ann, who was given a position as a maid at Charlecote Hall by the Lucy family, where she would learn her trade. She later earned a position as Sarah's live-in maid at Dial House Farm, Ashow on Tuesday, 21 March 1819.

Others have repeatedly written that sometime after Ann had taken up her new position with the Dormers, she had been caught at Dial House with bank notes in her possession belonging to the family. They also claim that she had been persuaded to take the notes by her brother, Thomas. These claims are based on nothing more than the false assumption that, as Thomas was hanged after Ann, he was therefore no good and must have been involved.

It has also been claimed that if not for Sarah speaking up for her, Ann would have surely been hanged. However, there is no record of the date that this crime was committed, nor proof that Ann had been arrested, imprisoned or tried for what was then the capital crime of 'Stealing in a Dwelling House', which came onto the statute by an Act of Parliament in 1713. This made it a capital crime to steal anything over the value of forty shillings.

So, when and to whom did Sarah speak in order for Ann to keep not only her life, but her position and home at Dial House? For example, five years earlier, Sarah Owens had been hanged for the same crime on 20 April 1814 at Ilchester, Somerset.

During Ann's trial, which we will come to later, this event was mentioned twice. First, it was mentioned that Sarah had saved Ann from the gallows by speaking up for her, but no other details are recorded. And second, Ann's trial judge did not permit evidence volunteered on her behalf showing that she had little or no reason to and would not have benefited from murdering Sarah, because it was regarding a 'past transgression'!

These were the words of Ann's trial judge over two hundred years ago. Now, it's time to open 'Pandora's box' for the truth to be finally known about this two-century-old cover-up.

In June and July 1819, Ann had fallen in love with Sarah's 20-year-old second eldest son, James Harris Dormer, and discovered that she was pregnant. Fearing that when Sarah and Joseph learned of the pregnancy, they would throw her out, leaving her with nowhere to go but back to her ill mother's in Charlecote with another hungry mouth to feed and no way of financially supporting themselves, Ann decided to take the bank notes. Her brother, Thomas, was totally innocent of any implication in this.

Having caught Ann with the bank notes, Sarah and Joseph agreed to charge Ann, fully aware of the dreadful consequences which would fall upon her if found guilty. Joseph rode off to Warwick Assizes where he formally made the charge against her, and then headed back home. It was during Joseph's absence when Sarah, bewildered by why Ann would need to steal from them, asked the young woman for her reason. It was then when Sarah had learnt the unexpected truth that Ann was pregnant with James' child.

Joseph arrived back home, completely ignorant to what Sarah had been told until she revealed that Ann was carrying their first grandchild. This left them in a predicament; if they continued with the charge against Ann, they would lose the child forever.

The only option was to arrange for the charge against Ann to be dropped, but this wouldn't be easy, as the Assizes treated false accusations with the same seriousness as the crime itself. It became clear that they would need help from someone they knew who had influence at the Assizes, but who? Joseph knew of only one person, and that was his landlord and the Warwick magistrate, the first Baron Leigh, Chandos, of Stoneleigh, who we will meet again, along with his solicitor, Thomas Denman.

The charge disappeared, and the next day Ann carried on with her normal duties as if nothing had happened, now safe in her mind that she would be looked after, at least until the child was born. But what of the child's father, James?

Back then, the 'guilty party' was sent away into temporary exile; but staying with family in Ashow would have local tongues wagging, especially with the villagers being aware of Ann's charge. Learning she had got away with it wouldn't have been received with much sympathy.

The only place which wasn't that far away and where James' presence wouldn't draw too much suspicion or require his absence from Dial House was in Leek Wootton with his cousin, James Lee Dormer, who we have already met, and his family. We will meet his children later.

This is the evidence Ann's trial judge hid from the court, which shows Ann would have had no reason to bite the hand that fed her. At the time of Sarah's murder, Ann was at least two months pregnant. Unfortunately, Ann would lose her child while in Warwick Gaol before her trial; the record of the child's birth and internment were also covered up.

Ann's mother, Mary, finally succumbed to her illness at home in Charlecote in early 1821, aged 71. She was reunited with her beloved husband and her first child on 22 February 1821 at St Leonard's Churchyard, leaving Hannah very much alone after her brother Thomas' execution. Shortly after her mother's death, Hannah left Charlecote and moved to Birmingham. On

Wednesday, 2 July 1823, she married John Cooper at St Martin's Church, Edgbaston, then aged 38.

In early January 1857, Hannah died, aged 73 and was buried at St Laurence Churchyard, Foleshill, Warwickshire on 18 January.

Chapter 3

'Murder, My Mother Is Murdered!'

Now, let's unfold the events of that fateful day in detail. We'll learn about each of the cast of characters involved. The murder of the 59-year-old farmer's wife and mother of six on the evening of Sunday, 29 August 1819 at Dial House Farm, Ashow, sent a shockwave through the local village and South Warwickshire. It would echo further afield when news broke that Sarah Dormer had been brutally murdered by her 21-year-old maidservant, Ann Heytrey, who was charged with the horrid crime of murder – petty treason. This described the killing of a superior by a subordinate, of a master or mistress by his or her servant, of a senior member of the clergy by a junior member, or of a husband by his wife – for which the price to pay was to be hanged.

This differed from the crime of treason, which was defined as a crime against the crown or state during the reign of Henry VIII, and resulted in the convicted being partially hanged, then being taken down to watch their insides and private parts be burned before their eyes, and afterwards the body was cut into quarters. Just one of the over 200 crimes back then which were classed as being capital offences within the aptly named Bloody Code.

Today, with over two centuries having passed, for the first time now armed with the transcript of the court report, including the witness statements and the surgeon and constable's reports, we can return to that fateful evening and re-examine what really happened. We can evaluate the events that resulted in the brutal murder of an innocent woman, laying almost decapitated on her own bedroom floor, and in doing so discover the truth – and lay ghosts to rest once and for all!

The now Grade II-listed Dial House Farm was built on the Stoneleigh Estate by the Leigh family around 1776. Additional out buildings, including the granary and wagon hovel, were added in 1800, and very little has changed as it stands today. It sits proud and isolated on a ridge about half a mile west of the ancient village of Ashow, on the boundary with Kenilworth, separated then by Thickthorn Woods, and today by the Kenilworth bypass.

The front of Dial House looks out onto the Stoneleigh Road (B4115) from the Chesford crossroads, between Leamington Spa and Kenilworth, some three miles south of the Warwickshire county town of Warwick. The ridge at the rear slopes down to the River Avon as it flows towards Ashow, over which the nearby fourteenth-century Chesford Bridge stands with the Leamington Spa-Kenilworth Road.

Sunday, 29 August 1819 wasn't just any normal Sunday for the residents of Ashow; it was their 'Wake' day. The English calendar then was littered with rural festive gatherings throughout the spring, summer and autumn. Depending on the part of the countryside where they were held, these events had a bewildering variety of names, such as fairs, fetes, revels, ales, treats, mops, and wakes, such as at Ashow on that day. These festivals would have drawn in visitors from as far afield as Coventry, some eight miles away.

As the sun rose and the Dormer household woke early, Ann was the first awake as she lit the fires and attended to Sarah. Outside in the farmyard, the three other family farm servants – 44-year-old Richard Smith, 31-year-old John Barnacle, and 9-year-old John Branstone – were busy with their duties, including the early morning milking.

Mr Dormer's horse was also being readied, as Joseph was leaving early this morning. After breakfast, Joseph rode off alone towards Coventry, where he had arranged to meet family friends and business associates of St Michael's, Coventry-born father and son, 54-year-old Jonathan and 24-year-old William Bray, maltsters and brewers.

Joseph took them to local farmers on a 'meet-and-greet', with the intention of persuading the farmers to change their crops from wheat to barley to supply the Brays, who would buy the crop at a cheaper price than on the open market. The Corn Laws had inflated the price of grain. After obtaining the barley, the Brays would germinate it in malthouses, such as the one in nearby Kenilworth, transforming it into malt, which they would use themselves in their own establishments, and sell on the surplus to other brewers in Coventry.

Joseph was not only a farmer but also seemingly an astute businessman, as he could see the advantages in the growing beer trade in Coventry. However, there was a knock-on effect – if local farmers increased their barley crop, it would come at the cost of reducing their wheat crop, which would drive up the price of bread. Alongside barley, bread was also heavily affected by the Corn Laws, so he may have even been seen by some as profiteering from the financial misery!

Meanwhile, back home, it was mid-morning when Sarah and her five children had received their two invited guests and family friends for lunch. The first was Weston-born and Stoneleigh resident 25-year-old Thomas Harris, the future husband of Sarah's eldest daughter, 23-year-old Elizabeth.[1] The second guest was Kenilworth-born and residing 26-year-old William Hinde.

It was around 2.00 pm when Joseph returned home with Jonathan and William Bray and had tea with the family, which both Sarah and Ann had prepared, and which Ann had served. About the same time as Joseph returned, the three farm servants were allowed to leave the farm to visit the village wake. Richard Smith stayed there all afternoon and never left until he returned to the farm at 8.20 pm with young John Branstone, who had returned for milking at 5 pm, but had returned to the wake at 5.30 pm. John Barnacle had returned to the farm at 3.45 pm before returning to the wake shortly afterwards. He finally returned to the farm at 7.45 pm.

At around 6.00 pm, Mr William Hinde and Sarah's children left Dial House and walked towards Kenilworth to visit Thomas and Mary (Lewis) Aldridge at nearby Thickthorn Lodge, a three-story farmhouse just south of Windy Arbour, a short walk away on the other side of Thickthorn Woods.[2]

At the same time as William Hinde and the children left Dial House, Joseph Dormer, accompanied by Jonathan Bray, William Bray, and Thomas Harris also left and were seen off at the front gate by Sarah for the village wake, leaving Sarah and Ann alone on the farm. Unknown to Joseph, that would be the last time he would see his wife alive.

At around 6.30 pm, there was a knock on the back door, which Ann had answered to discover 11-year-old Ann Maria Lee Dormer, and her 9-year-old brother, Joseph Lee Dormer, the children of James Lee Dormer, who we have already met. The children were invited in and given a glass of wine and a cucumber snack. Others have claimed the reason for the children turning up at the back door of Dial House was that they were 'scavenging'. Nothing could be further from the truth, as it was Joseph's birthday; thus the reason why he had visited his great-aunt that day.[3]

Just before 7.00 pm, Leek Wootton-born and residing 26-year-old Elizabeth Jaggard[4] was riding past the front of Dial House on her way to visit her friend, Ashow-born 29-year-old Jane Russell,[5] at Forge Cottage in the village.

As Elizabeth was passing, she saw Sarah sat in her chair reading with her spectacles on through the ground floor middle window. And at the same time, she saw Ann, dressed in a red gown, cap and apron, walk from around the back of the house and come out into the lane in front of her and look down it towards the direction of the village.

Ann immediately returned to the back of the house. Elizabeth believed that Ann hadn't noticed her; she also confirmed that Ann was the same woman who she had witnessed later that evening being helped on to the back of a cart by the local constable, as she had passed Dial House on her way back home.

At 7.10 pm, William Hinde and Sarah's children returned to Dial House from Thickthorn, and found the front door shut but not locked. Elizabeth was the first to enter and found Ann at the end of the hallway by the opened back door. Ann appeared to her to be much agitated and was perspiring very much. Elizabeth had asked Ann if anyone had been in the house since they had left, Ann replied, 'No, nobody.'

Ann then went out the back door into the back garden and down to the wood pile, before returning almost immediately. Upon Ann's return, Elizabeth believed that she still looked very confused. It was during Ann's short absence when Elizabeth had noticed blood spots on the hallway floor. Elizabeth questioned Ann, asking what had she been doing, to which Ann had replied, 'Oh nothing'.

By now Elizabeth had been joined in the hallway by her sisters, Harriet and Mary. Meanwhile, her brothers Joseph and John were outside in the farmyard by the court pailing. Ann was then asked where their mother was. Her answer was disputed during Ann's trial, as Harriet and Mary contradicted each other by claiming that Ann had given two different replies. Firstly, that Sarah had gone out into the back garden to collect cucumbers about ten minutes ago, and secondly, that she had gone out towards Ashow.

Becoming increasingly concerned, Harriet began calling out to her mother, and without receiving any reply, Elizabeth began to climb the stairs, with Mary following her. Elizabeth walked past her mother's door and went into her own bedroom at the end of the landing. Mary opened her mother's door and found Sarah lying on her back on the floor, her heels pointing towards the door. She screamed out 'Murder, murder, my mother is murdered!' Mary would claim later that when she had discovered her mother, she hadn't seen any blood.

One of the first to react to Mary's scream was her brother Joseph, who ran into one of the barns and grabbed a pitchfork before running into the house and upstairs, with Ann following him. Seeing his mother lying on the floor, he turned and grabbed Ann by her arm and dragged her downstairs and out of the house into the lane at the front, where he accused her of murdering his mother. In a fit of rage, he struck Ann on her left cheek. Joseph would later claim that when he had accused Ann of murdering his mother, she had given no reply.

Others who were passing the house and were drawn to it by the young girl's scream was Kenilworth surgeon Dr William Bodington,[6] who rode up to the front door. After dismounting, he was directed upstairs and into Sarah's bedroom. William examined Sarah and found a deep wound to her throat. He also noticed a knife between her hand and arm, and her side, but not grasped in her clenched hand. He didn't open her hand, but he had no doubt that the deep wound to Sarah's throat was the cause of her death.

William then sealed up Sarah's door until the next morning, leaving strict instructions that no one was to open it. As William had entered, Harriet had run out of the house and began running down the lane towards the village to tell her father the dreadful news, with William Hinde following closely behind her.

Another who had been passing Dial House and was drawn to it by Mary's scream was Kenilworth-born local clothes dealer, and later, comb manufacturer, 30-year-old Henry Beesley.[7] Henry had entered the house, and after finding a light, had traced the blood spots on the floor to the best kitchen,[8] the room where Sarah had been seen sat by the window reading by Ms Elizabeth Jaggard just before 7.00 pm. Upon entering the room, Henry observed a pair of spectacles on the floor by the window, and a book on the table.

The third person and witness who heard Mary's scream as he was passing the house was William (Dormer) Pope.[9] William didn't enter the house, but had stood on the lane directly opposite. William witnessed Joseph drag Ann out into the lane in front of him, where he heard her protest that Joseph need not drag her, as she would go where he took her.

He also heard Joseph accuse her of his mother's murder and heard her reply that she hadn't, and watched as he struck her. William had approached Ann afterwards, sympathetically asking her if she had seen anyone about the house, no was her reply, and if she had left the house, 'Yes,' she replied, 'To the wood pile.'

It wouldn't have taken Harriet more than ten minutes to run from Dial House down to the village to inform her father of her mother's death. Upon hearing the dreadful news, a rider was sent to inform the local constable of Sarah's murder.

At around 8.30 pm, the Kenilworth constable, Yorkshire-born 33-year-old Thomas Bellerby,[10] arrived at Dial House and found Ann standing by the front gate with Ashow-born local boot and shoemaker, 44-year-old Samuel Turner.[11]

After dismounting from his horse and cart, Thomas approached Ann and asked if she was the young woman who had been charged with the murder of Mrs Sarah Dormer, she replied, 'They say so, but I am not.'

Thomas noted that Ann was wearing a red gown, and a sort of hurden (i.e., coarse) apron, that the left side of her face was much swelled, and that her hands looked bloody as if they had been wiped, though the apron she had been wearing was free of blood.

Constable Bellerby took Ann into custody. Before he helped her onto the back of his cart, he had asked her if the apron she was wearing was the one she had worn earlier on in the afternoon. She replied that it was not, and that she had changed it with another, the original which she had hung up on the back door. As Ann climbed into the back of the cart, Elizabeth Jaggard rode past on her way home, and confirmed that it was the same young woman who she had seen come out into the lane earlier. Ann was then carted off to Warwick Gaol, from where she would never leave. From the first moment she had entered, her fate was sealed.

Footnotes

1. Mr Thomas Harris and Elizabeth Dormer were married at St Mary the Virgin Church in Stoneleigh on 29 October 1822, by the curate, A.C. Morrison. Their two witnesses were Elizabeth's youngest brother, John, and her sister, Harriet. They set up home in the nearby 202-acre Dale House Farm, where on 29 June 1863, Thomas died.
2. Thomas Davis Aldridge, the son of William and Katherine, was born in Solihull in 1776, where he was baptized locally on 9 October. Thomas and Mary Lewis were married in Hampton-in-Arden on 14 April 1801, and it was shortly afterwards when they moved into Thickthorn, which had begun as a cottage in the imperial period, and by 1811 had become a manor house in the mock Tudor style.

   In 1830, Thomas had begun to make even more costly improvements by adding castellations, turrets and an even more elaborately ornate gatehouse, which resulted in Thomas becoming bankrupt. However, he hatched a plan to retain Thickthorn.

   On 7 December 1830, Thomas visited his solicitor, Worcestershire-born 28-year-old Mr Samuel William Haynes, in Warwick, along with his son Robert Aldridge, and Kenilworth local surgeon Dr William Bodington, who we will meet again very shortly. Thomas transferred the deeds of Thickthorn, its stable, and its four-and-a-half acres of gardens jointly over to both Robert and William.

On 30 December 1830, Thomas travelled to London, where on that day he declared himself bankrupt. After returning home later the following month, he, Robert and William returned to Thomas' solicitor, where the deeds of Thickthorn were returned to him.

Thomas would remain at Thickthorn for a further four years until his death in late March 1835, aged 58, and was laid to rest at St Nicholas Churchyard, Kenilworth, on 4 April.

This author completely understands the love that Thomas held for Thickthorn. It was where my parents first met and where we had lived while my late father had been employed as the gamekeeper and head gardener between 1970 and 1974.

3. We have already discovered that James Lee Dormer was the illegitimate son of Joseph Dormer's younger sister, Anna Maria Dormer. James Lee Dormer married Warwick-born Elizabeth Hobbins at All Saints Church, Leek Wootton on 11 January 1808, with her banns being read out back home in Warwick at St Nicholas Church, a stone's throw from the walls of Warwick Castle.

   James and Elizabeth settled in Leek Wotton where their first child, Ann Maria Lee Dormer, named after Elizabeth's mother, was born the following year, and baptized locally at All Saints Church on 20 November 1809.

   Two years later, Elizabeth would give birth to twins, Joseph Lee and Harriet Lee Dormer, who were baptized together locally on 29 August 1811. However, only two years later, in 1813, tragedy would strike for the first time, but sadly not the last, when young Harriet died, aged 2 years and 3 months, and was buried at All Saints Church by the curate, Thomas Clarke, on 2 October 1813.

At the time of Harriet's death, Elizabeth was seven months pregnant with James Edmond Lee Dormer. The shock of losing Harriet caused Elizabeth to give birth prematurely in May 1814. Due to James being born early, his chance of survival was known to be limited, and as such Joseph and Elizabeth decided instead of him being baptized locally, they would take him to St Michael's, the family ancestral church in Coventry, where he was baptized on 27 May 1814.

Only a few weeks after their return, their greatest fear came to pass. Young James died and was buried by curate Thomas Clarke, the same who had buried Harriet only the year before. James was buried alongside Harriet at All Saints Church on 17 June 1814. Elizabeth died at home in late June 1822 and was buried locally on 30 June.

4. Elizabeth Jaggard was born in Leek Wootton in 1793 and baptized locally on 19 September. She was the only surviving child of local-born horse breeder William and his wife Hannah Jaggard. In early 1792, Hannah had given birth to their first child, Thomas, who had died at just fifteen weeks old and was buried locally at All Saints Church. Their third child, after Elizabeth, Abraham, was born in 1807 and died the following year on 12 April

1808, aged eleven months. Three years later, her father William died on 11 March 1811, aged 47.

On 31 March 1825, Elizabeth married William Umbers at All Saints Church in Leek Wootton. They remained in Leek Wootton to look after her mother until Hannah's death on 23 April 1836, aged 69. After Hannah's death, the couple left Leek Wootton and moved to Wappenbury, where on 11 September 1850, Elizabeth died at home, aged 57, and was buried locally on 14 September.

5. Elizabeth's friend at Forge Cottage in Ashow, Jane Russell, was born in Stoneleigh in 1790, where she was baptized at St Mary the Virgin Church on 30 December. Jane would later leave Ashow and move to nearby Kenilworth, where at St Nicholas Church she would marry Thomas Carter on 8 January 1821.
6. Dr William Bodington FRCS was born in Kenilworth in 1790, the son of Joseph and Mary (Cattell) Bodington, who were married in Knowle near Kenilworth on 3 December 1786. Mary's brother, and William's uncle, Joseph Cattell, would be Ann's jury foreman at the trial the following year.

William was educated at the London Hospital, where on 6 May 1808 he passed his MRCS and became a member of the Royal College of Surgeons. On 9 December 1852, he passed his FRCS.

William married his cousin, Kenilworth-born 24-year-old Eliza Draper at St Nicholas Church, Kenilworth, on 10 September 1812, the daughter of Cartwright and Elizabeth (Adkins) Draper. William and Eliza set up home and his practice in Kenilworth at Montague House on Upper Rosemary Hill. After Ann's execution, he would dissect her there in the back garden. William died at home on 17 October 1872, aged 82, and was buried locally at St Nicholas Church on 23 October.

7. Henry Beesley was born in Kenilworth in late 1791, where he was baptized at St Nicholas Church on 15 January 1792, the son of Henry and Elizabeth Beesley. Henry married Bagington-born 29-year-old Ms Sarah Pratt at St Nicholas Church, Kenilworth. They set up home on the High Street in Kenilworth until around 1861, when they had moved to Warwick Street in Rugby.
8. Back then, houses like Dial House were built with two kitchens. The back kitchen was where servants would cook meals, and the second, the best kitchen, was at the front where the family would live – what we now call living rooms.
9. William (Dormer) Pope was born in Kenilworth in 1792, and baptized later that year at St Nicholas Church on 23 October, the son of Mr Thomas Dormer and Ms Sarah Pope. Thomas Dormer is a bit of an enigma; however, his mother, Sarah, was born in Kenilworth in 1768 and baptized at St Nicholas Church on 9 September.

   Sarah was the daughter of Charles and Sarah Pope; her father died in late October 1797 and was buried at St Nicholas Church on 2 November. Her mother joined her father at St Nicholas on 25 October 1807.

William (Dormer) Pope, who had chosen his mother's maiden name over his father's, died on 26 July 1826, aged 37.

10. Constable Thomas Bellerby was born in the Yorkshire village of Ousebridge, York, in 1786, where he was baptized at St John's Church on 27 August, the son of John and Mary (Retallack) Bellerby. Having completed his education locally, Thomas was apprenticed to John Fothergill, an ivory and comb manufacturer of Holy Trinity, Micklegate, York on 16 July 1799, aged just 13.
11. Samuel Turner was born in Ashow in early 1777 and was baptized locally on 16 March, the son of Jess and Mary Turner. On 16 October 1801, Samuel married Mary Reynolds at St Nicholas Church, Kenilworth, where they set up home at 46 Mill End.

    Several years after his mother's death, Sarah's youngest, John Dormer, would serve his apprenticeship as a boot and shoemaker under Samuel. Afterwards, John would take over The Boot Inn on Castle Street in Kenilworth, where he would apply his trade as well as being the innkeeper. Samuel died in late October 1852 and was buried locally in St Nicholas' Churchyard on 1 November.

    Having completed his apprenticeship, Thomas was assigned to William Chippendale as a joiner until 3 August 1818, when for whatever reason Thomas left Yorkshire, moved to Kenilworth, and joined the local Constabulary.

On 18 April 1821, Thomas married Maria Hollis at St George's Church, Hanover Square, Westminster in London. Maria was the daughter of John and Mrs Elizabeth Hollis. Maria was born in Westminster in 1798, where she was baptized at St James' Church on 18 November later that year.

After their marriage, Thomas and Maria returned to Kenilworth, where he continued as the local constable, and where on 11 May 1823 their first child, Mary, was born. By 1840, Thomas had been promoted and had moved to Warwick, where he and Mary resided in Theatre Street, and where their second daughter, named after her mother, Maria, was born. Eight years later, tragedy struck when during an outbreak of cholera in Warwick, two of its many victims were Thomas's wife and youngest daughter, 42-year-old Maria and 8-year-old Maria, who were taken the same day, and were buried together locally on 3 May 1848 at the Collegiate Church of St Mary's.

By 1848, Thomas' eldest daughter, Mary, had left Warwick and moved to London, where she learnt of her father's death on 8 February 1851. Thomas, who had become the chief constable of Kenilworth and then the superintendent of police for Warwick, died at home aged 64. He joined his wife and youngest daughter at the Collegiate Church of St Mary's four days after on 12 February, a stone's throw from the front of Warwick Gaol on Northgate Street – it was its bell that had tolled for Ann as she had climbed the steps of the gallows.

Eight months after her father's death, Mary married William Boulton, sculptor, at St George the Martyr Church, Southwark in London on 13 October 1851. Two years later, Mary was taken by cholera in 1853, aged 30.

Chapter 4

Ann's Confession

Now, we'll go over the official events of the next day, including the constable's taking of Ann's confession. The following morning, Constable Thomas Bellerby returned to Dial House to carry out his investigation. He was met by Kenilworth surgeon Dr William Bodington and his colleague and fellow surgeon, Dr William Hiron of Southam, who had also returned to examine Sarah's body. Thomas left the two surgeons in Sarah's bedroom while he went outside into the back garden looking for clues.

Rolled up on the floor of the shed outside of the back door, he discovered a blood-stained apron. In a large washtub by the back gate, he discovered another blood-stained apron and hand towel soaking at the bottom of the soapy water, underneath other towels, none of which were stained with blood.

Meanwhile, upstairs in Sarah's bedroom, the two surgeons had completed their examination of her, and wrote a report that was read out in court the following year at Ann's trial:

> 'Her (Sarah's) throat was cut violently so as to divide all the parts of her spine – the spine had been cut more than once – there were two deep cuts on her left jaw, one of them extended to her mouth – there were several small scratches on the left side of her face, and a violent bruise on her nose – that one of her teeth was knocked out from her upper jaw, also another from her lower jaw opposite the former – there were several bruises on various areas of her body – the middle finger of her left hand had been cut deeply across in two places, and there were other cuts on the fingers of both hands. The first cut to the spine would have been fatal – it was impossible for the deceased to have inflicted the wounds on herself – it was utterly impossible. The fingers of the deceased were cut on the right hand and the tendons divided, as if she had caught at the knife.'

Having completed their examination, the two surgeons left Dial House, leaving Constable Bellerby able to go into the house and upstairs into Sarah's bedroom, where she lay with the knife still by her side. Thomas lifted her shoulders. Underneath one shoulder, he found her blood-stained black cap, which he believed would have been worn under another, and underneath the other, he found a piece of blood-stained flannel. Sarah's white cap was on her head, which would have been worn over her black cap.

Later that day, Thomas had ridden to Warwick Gaol and had interviewed Ann in her cell, informing her that he had apprehended her brother, Thomas, for his concern in Sarah's murder. Ann responded by saying, 'What a thing it was to bring my friends into trouble, neither my brother or no man had to do with it.' Thomas replied by saying, 'If you say that, you know who did it.' Ann responded, 'I did it, and no one helped me'. With her last statement, little did she know then that she had sealed her fate.

Now, for the first time having confessed to Sarah's murder, Ann was asked by Thomas for her own account of the events of that evening. Ann said that after the family had left the house, she and Sarah were alone. Later, the two children had arrived, but left shortly afterwards, again leaving her and Sarah alone in the house. After the children had left, they both went out into the back garden to collect cucumbers for the family's supper later.

Having collected the cucumbers, they both returned to the back kitchen, when Ann took them into the adjacent pantry and began to chop them up with a few onions. Sarah walked up the hallway and into the best kitchen, where she sat in her chair, put her spectacles on, and began to read from her book.

It was while Ann was chopping up the vegetables that the thought came into her head that she must murder Sarah. She put the knife down, came out of the pantry into the back kitchen, changed her apron, and walked out into the back garden and down to the woodpile. She then returned to the back of the house before going out to the front and into the lane, returning to the back kitchen almost immediately.

Upon entering the back door, she had walked up the hallway and into the best kitchen where Sarah was still sat reading, book in hand, and knocked her out of her chair and onto the floor. Ann had stood over Sarah as she lay on the floor for about a minute, before Sarah had gotten up and run out of the room, along the hallway, upstairs, and into her bedroom. Ann followed Sarah out of the room and stopped halfway down to go into the dairy, where she picked up the carving knife before following Sarah upstairs and into her bedroom.

Ann said that as she entered Sarah's bedroom, she had found her lying on the floor, believing that Sarah may have tripped on the carpet or had fainted, 'but she hadn't knocked her down'. She had then leant over her and began cutting her with the carving knife. Sarah gave little or no resistance until she had been cut two or three times. Sarah never spoke, but gave a rustling noise, and caught at the knife with her hands. Ann had then held Sarah down until she was dead, and then put the white cap back on her head which had come off during the struggle, before placing the knife by her side.

With Ann having made her confession, Thomas then asked her, 'Why didn't you put the black cap back on her head?' Ann replied, 'I didn't think about it.' Thomas then asked, 'Why did you put the knife by her side?' Ann said, 'I lifted Sarah's arm and put it there, because I wanted others to believe that she had done it herself.'

Thomas then asked, 'How did the bloody towel found in the tub get there?' Ann responded, 'I had put it there, and meant to have washed it out the following morning.' Thomas followed up with, 'Where did you get the towel from?' Ann responded that she 'had taken it off the banister leading from Sarah's room as soon as I came from it, and wiped my hands on it.'

The constable asked, 'Can you explain the piece of bloody flannel found under Sarah's shoulder?' 'I had taken it, wiped my hands on it and threw it down, and just forgot about it,' said Ann. Thomas then asked, 'How did blood get on the hurden apron?' Ann said, 'I cannot tell.'

Mrs Sarah Dormer was buried in the Assumption of Our Lady churchyard, Ashow, on Wednesday, 1 September 1819. Going by the church burial records, Sarah was aged 56 at the time of her death, which would mean she was born in 1763, which would have been some three years after her actual baptism. Sarah would be reunited with her husband, Joseph Dormer, when he was buried on Saturday, 15 May 1830. A headstone was erected in memory of both, with Joseph's correct age at death recorded.

However, on the present headstone, Sarah is recorded as being aged 47 at the time of her death in 1819 – some twelve years out from her actual age, and nine years from the age recorded in the church burial records. At the time of Joseph's death, when the headstone was being erected, if Sarah's age was unknown, surely all it would have taken was for her children to check the burial records. Then, the headstone would have been only three years out from her real age instead of the twelve years as it now stands. There can be only two explanations: Sarah's eldest children, Elizabeth (Dormer) Harris and Joseph Dormer, didn't care, or this was done deliberately!

Chapter 5

Murder, the Law, and Warwick Gaol

Let's take a few moments to understand the law of the land and punishments at the time this crime occurred, and to get a picture of what being incarcerated in Warwick Gaol would have been like. Ann was charged with murder–petty treason, one of over 200 capital offences on the statute at the time, for which the penalty was to be boarded upon a hurdle to the place of execution. The poor unfortunate would be hanged, and after the appropriate time had been given, cut down, and their body handed over to the Surgeon's Hall for dissection.

Hanging in Britain was first introduced by the Anglo Saxons during the fifth century as the principal method of execution. However, there were other more imaginative forms being used, including drowning, beheading, burning at the stake, shooting, boiling alive, hurling from cliffs, and being buried alive.

In 1351, the Treason Act of King Edward III defined the crimes of high treason and petty treason in law, for which the punishment was to be hanged, drawn and quartered – a rather nasty and vindictive form of punishment. It involved the perpetrator being partially hanged by the neck, then taken down and laid on a flat surface while his or her private parts were cut off and burnt before their eyes. After which, while they were still alive, their entrails were cut out and also burnt, before their body was divvied into four parts.

Around 1540, during the reign of King Henry VIII, there were eleven capital crimes defined as high treason: counterfeiting coin, petty treason, murder, rape, piracy, arson of a dwelling house or barn with corn in it, highway robbery, embezzling one's master's goods, horse theft, robbing churches, and robbing a person in a dwelling house. Two years later, witchcraft was added, and was punishable by hanging in England versus burning in Scotland, which would be repealed in 1547 by Edward VI.

On 29 July 1563, Queen Elizabeth I reclassed witchcraft as being a capital offence, which would remain on the statute until around 1736, when it was repealed by King James I in Scotland. But witch hunting continued even as late as 14 February 1945, when the body of 74-year-old Charles Walton was discovered on Meon Hill, Lower Quinton, Warwickshire, with his throat cut and his body pinned to the ground by a pitchfork.

Warwickshire Police had gotten nowhere with the investigation into Charles' murder, and so Detective Superintendent Robert Fabian of Scotland Yard was sent to investigate. However, Robert faced a local population that closed ranks, little trusting to his intent, so at the end he was recalled without getting any further in discovering the culprit of the murder than those who had preceded him.

Robert Fabian (Fabian of the Yard) later wrote a book about the murder of Mr Walton and his attempted investigation, in which he clearly indicates that he believed that witchcraft was involved. And if you should find yourself on Meon Hill in Lower Quinton on a late evening, keep a watchful eye out for a black dog. Don't worry, it won't bite – it can't!

On 30 January 1649, King Charles I was wrongfully and unlawfully beheaded at Whitehall for treason, the only English king to be executed in England. Later that year on 23 June, the largest number of common criminals were put to death at one time at Tyburn when twenty-three men and one woman were drawn to the gallows by eight carts to be hanged for burglary and robbery.

It was common back then for the criminals to be carted from the local gaol, where they had been held, and to stop off at every inn en route to the gallows. At each stop, they were given either wine or beer to ease their entry into the other world.

On 26 August 1685, what came to be known as the Bloody Assizes began in response and aftermath of the Monmouth Rebellion, when over 320 men and women were put to death. The men were mostly hanged, drawn and quartered. Its first victim was 67-year-old Lady Alice Lisle, who was beheaded at Winchester on

2 September for treason, having been caught sheltering two traitors.

1713 saw an Act of Parliament define the crime of stealing in a dwelling house as a capital offence in the value of forty shillings (£2), which we know that Ann had fallen foul of just a few months before Sarah's death.

In 1718, Parliament passed the Transportation Act, which allowed courts to reduce the sentences of criminals found guilty of non-capital offences to allow them to be sent to America for seven years; offenders of capital offences could be sent for fourteen years to life. This ceased in 1775 due to the start of the American War of Independence, and as a result, the number of executions rose significantly between 1775 and 1786. During the same period, London saw an explosion in the number of murders.

In 1751, Parliament passed an act 'For better preventing the horrid crime of murder'. It laid down the rules for the treatment of those who were convicted of murder. This included that those convicted were to be kept in chains in isolation and fed on bread and water, and should be hanged within forty-eight hours of their conviction unless it fell on a Sunday, when it was to be delayed until the following day (Monday).

It also decreed that after execution, the body would be sent for dissection or gibbeting, which only applied to men and meant that their body would be hung up near the scene of their crime in a metal-framed cage. Suspended thirty feet in the air from either a tree or gibbeting post, the body was left to rot, sometimes for decades. Once the bones had fallen through the gibbet, they were to be buried at the base of the tree or post.

It also specified that the bodies were prevented from being buried in consecrated ground, thus punishing not only the criminal in the afterlife, but also their families by denying them the right of a religious burial. The Act came into being on 1 June 1752 as the Murder Act, and its first victim was 17-year-old murderer Thomas Woolford, who was hanged at Tyburn on 22 June and then dissected (anatomized) at the Surgeons' Hall.

On 8 March 1784, Mary Bailey became the last person to be burned at the stake for petty treason, for the murder of her husband at Winchester. Four years later in 1788, transportation resumed to Australia, which would reduce the executions from 434 hangings in just the London area between 1784 and 1793 to 165 over the following decade. Up until 1868, over 162,000 men, women and children were transported to Australia.

The barbaric punishment of burning women at the stake for high and petty treason finally ended on 5 June 1790. The practice was replaced by being boarded upon a hurdle to the place of execution by hanging. For its last victim, it came one year too late, when on 18 March 1789, Catherine (Bowman) Murphy was burnt at the stake at Newgate for coining–high treason.

By 1810, there were over 220 capital offences within English and Welsh law, whereas there were only around twenty in Scottish law. Four years after, the Treason Act of 1814 removed the requirement of disembowelling and quartering for men convicted of high treason.

Ann would spend seven months in Warwick Gaol before her trial at Warwick Assizes next door on Northgate Street.[1]

Warwick has a long and bloody history, which began within the walls of the finest English Norman Castle, where prisoners were held in its dungeon and tried in its great hall. If found guilty, they were loaded on the back of carts and driven to their place of execution on nearby Gallows Hill.

Today, Heathcote Industrial Estate stands on Gallows Hill. Several years back, my late friend, who worked night security on the factory floor, witnessed an apparition of a bedraggled male figure with his hands chained in front of him being dragged across the floor.

By 1600, a new prison had been built on the junction of today's Northgate Street and Barrack Street. In 1694, during the Great Fire of Warwick that swept through the town, it burnt down. By the early 1700s, it had been rebuilt, and further additions were added during the century. The gaol as it now stands, next door to the old Shire Hall, hasn't changed much from the evening when Ann walked in. She would be the last of eighteen women to be publicly hanged at Warwick between 1739 and 1820. The other seventeen were:

Mary Britain, on Friday, 13 April 1739, for the murder of her child; buried at St Mary's Church, Warwick, on 16 April.

Anne (Morrell) Morrill, on Thursday, 12 August 1762, for the murder of her child; buried at St Mary's Church, Warwick, on 12 August.

Hannah Saunders, in summer 1775, for highway robbery.

On 20 August 1778, the only occasion when two women were publicly hanged together at Warwick: Alice Curtis, for murder of her bastard child. Mary (Wright) Knight, for murder of her youngest son, 5-year-old Roger, after beating the boy to death with a stick at home in Chilvers Cotton, Nuneaton, and throwing his body down a well. It was evidence by 8-year-old William, her eldest son, that sealed his mother's fate.

Elizabeth (Kennard) Green, on Friday, 22 April 1785, for stealing in a dwelling house; buried at St Martin's Churchyard, Birmingham, on 24 April.

Eleanor Haywood, on Monday, 3 April 1786, for murder of her bastard child.

Ann Sutton, on Saturday, 15 April 1786, for theft.

Ann Cooke, on Friday, 26 April 1793, for highway robbery, alongside her male accomplice, Bickley Barnes.

Margaret Boulker, on Friday, 14 August 1795, for rioting and breaking a window of a steam mill with a stone in Birmingham.

The only brother and sister to be publicly hanged together at Warwick: On 1 April 1801, 21-year-old Snitterfield, Warwickshire-born Hannah Palmer and her 27-year-old brother, John Palmer, were hanged for the Wednesday, 1 January 1801 murder of John's wife, 26-year-old Oxfordshire-born Mary (French) Palmer. Hannah and John had led Mary out into a cornfield under false pretences, where they cut her throat and threw her naked body, wrapped in a winnowing sheet, into the River Avon. John was gibbeted, hung from a tree near to Binton-on-Avon Bridge, and left to rot; afterwards his remains were buried at the base of the tree. Hannah fared little better, as she was dissected.

Sarah Claridge, on 7 August 1801, for murder of her 4-year-old son; dissected.

Mary Lappidge, on 15 April 1803, for uttering forgery.[2]

Susannah Grant, on 18 August 1809, for high treason–coining,[3] buried at St Paul's Churchyard, Birmingham, the same day.

Ann Hawtin, on Monday, 14 April 1817, for murder of her newborn child; dissected.

Ann (Morris) Bamford, on 24 April 1818, for uttering, buried at St Peter and St Paul's Churchyard, Birmingham, on 28 April. At the time of Ann's execution, three of her children, Elizabeth, Rebecca, and William, were on their way to Australia after being convicted and sentenced to transportation. Ann is believed to have had one of the first all-female juries, which contradicts modern bleeding-heart historians' straight out from the factory, as they claim that this didn't occur before 1920! At her trial, her jury members were: Elizabeth Hobbis (fore-matron), Mary Hobbis, Martha Pickett, Susannah Claridge, Eliza Jordan, Theresa Franklin, Sarah Price, Mary Squires, Ann Betts, Mary Canning, Maria Hobbis, and Martha Godfrey. The trial judge was William Garrow, of the TV series *Garrows' Law.*

Mary (Leak) Bissaker, on Friday, 23 April 1819, for high treason–coining. 56-year-old Birmingham-born Mary was hanged on the nineteenth anniversary of her husband John's execution for the same crime on Whitley Common, Coventry, on 23 April 1800. Mary's body was returned to Birmingham, where she was buried on 27 April in St Mary's Churchyard, Whittall Street, Edgbaston.

Back to Ann: it was unknown to her, as she was led into Warwick Gaol and greeted by the gaoler, Mr Henry Tattnall,[4] that she would be number eighteen, as well as the last woman, to be publicly hanged at Warwick – but not the first allegedly innocent to have been so.

During Ann's seven-month incarceration in Warwick Gaol, she had given birth in the most horrendous conditions, which there can be very little doubt resulted in the death of her child shortly after birth. The record of the child's birth and burial have been erased from history, as if he or she never existed.

To truly understand the dreadful and inhumane conditions in Warwick Gaol at that time, which Ann and her fellow felons had to endure, we need to refer back to a previous gaol inspection conducted on 15 February 1788:

'The felons were sadly crowded. Only one day-room for the men, and I saw thirty-two lie chained in a dungeon of twenty-two feet diameter, down thirty-one steps, two of whom were ill of a slow fever. There were three others in a room, very ill, and in irons. In two rooms seven feet-and-a-half by six-and-a-half with apertures only in the doors, there lay fourteen women, almost suffocated. None of the women were now in irons, no infirmary, no bath. "The Act of Preserving the Health of Prisoners" not hung up. No coals, no coals being allowed, the women here, as in other gaols, sell even their bread to procure fuel. Allowance, a three-pound loaf every other day, it was good bread and full weight.'

The inspection doesn't mention children directly, as they weren't recorded as children, but deliberately and shamefully hidden within the recorded numbers of felons and convicts. We already know that some of these infants and children were the unfortunate discarded offspring of prostitutes. Others were the children of those who had been banished by transportation, or who had been executed. The sad truth was that many didn't want to leave, as it was the only home they had ever known, or would ever know, despite all that faced them – so much for white privilege!

In 1824, 'Under the Provisions of the Act of King George IV' was transmitted to the secretary of state from the several counties, cities, and towns in England and Wales; it was commonly called 'The Gaol Act'. Gaols were required to send to the government returns proving that they were complying with the Act, and also the recommendations they made as to comply, if they hadn't been already. Warwick returned theirs on 14 October 1823, which was published on 10 March 1824.

This return was headed by the high sheriff of Warwickshire, Sir John Eardley Eardley-Wilmot, baronet (1783–1847), who we have already met, and also more interestingly, member of Parliament for Warwickshire, Sir Grey Skipworth, eighth baronet (1771–1852), the chairman of the quarter sessions of Alveston Villa, near Stratford-upon-Avon. Sir Grey was a direct descendant through his mother, Anne Miller, of the Native American Indian princess Pocahontas. It was Sir Grey's groom, William Sutton, who had discovered keys belonging to William Hiron on 4 November 1820 on Little Ham Bridge, Alveston, where he had been attacked; for his murder, Ann's brother, Thomas Heytrey, would hang on the same gallows as she had, the year after Ann, in 1821.

The 1824 return shows some significant improvements in the care of prisoners at Warwick from the 1788 inspection:

County of Warwick: Common Gaol.

23- 'Dietary or other Weekly Allowances; and Weekly costs per Head? --- Each prisoner receives ten pounds and three-quarters of Bread per Week, at 2d per pound, and Meat and Vegetables 6d. Weekly Cost, per Head, 2s. 3.1/2 d.'

24- 'Allowance of Clothing and Bedding, and Cost per Head? --- THE whole Suit of Clothing, Bedding, &c 4d, 4s, when new.'

26- 'Hours of Labour and Exercise? --- A.M. Labour from half past Six till Nine; then Prayers and Breakfast; Labour from half past Nine till One, then Dinner and Exercise. P.M. Labour from Two till Five, then Prayers and Exercise till Six.'

29- 'What duties are performed by the Chaplin, what Provision made for Instruction, and whether Prisoners are supplied with Bibles and other Books? --- THE Chaplin has hitherto performed Devine Service on Sundays and Fridays. A Schoolmaster instructs the Boys. Bibles and Prayer Books are supplied.'

30- 'Attendance of the Surgeon, and whether separate Buildings or Apartments are provided for the Sick? --- A SURGEON attends almost daily, and when required. A Sick Room for the Female Prisoners, and one for the Male Prisoners, nearly ready for use.'

34- 'General Observations --- A MATRON is constantly in attendance upon the Female Prisoners.'

(Signed) Henry Tatnall, Keeper.

At the time, Henry was still the gaoler (keeper) of Warwick Gaol, but now had six officers under his direction. It is fairly clear by the use of capital letters in his replies to the questions that he wasn't happy – almost screaming out. It's understandable that he had decided to retire shortly afterwards.

The second part of the return (magistrates to government) covered the House of Correction (Bridewell). It was built in 1687, succumbed to the same fate that befell the gaol during the 1694 Great Fire, and was rebuilt in the late eighteen century. It was located on the now-junction of Theatre and Barrack Streets across from the gaol, where a car park now stands.

At the time of the return, the house of correction was staffed by one keeper, two officers, one taskmaster, one miller, and one baker, all of whom were appointed by the then-keeper, Mr Joseph Chaplin:

> 23- 'Dietary or other Weekly Allowances; and Weekly Cost per Head? --- TWO pounds of Bread each daily. Weekly Cost, 2s, 4d, per head.'
>
> 24- 'Allowance of Clothing and Bedding, and Cost per Head?--- STRAW Beds, one Blanket, one Rug to each, Clothing allowed to those who cannot do without it. Cost per Head about 18s per annum on an average.'
>
> 25- 'Description of Employment, and Hard Labour? --- HARD Labour, grinding corn, Wire-drawing, heading Pins. No other Employment.'
>
> 26- 'Hours of Labour and of Exercise? --- NINE hours Labour, and two hours of Exercise.'
>
> 27- 'Amount of Earnings, how Applied, and in what Proportion to each Class of Prisoner, to the Officers of the Prison, and to the Fund applicable to the Maintenance of the said Prison? --- EARNING about 111 (eligible) per annum, from Wire-drawing and Pin-heading (not money

to the County) paid to the County Treasurer. Prisoners receive about two-pence in a shilling upon their Earnings. Officers do not receive any thing from the Prisoners Earnings. Prisoners allowed 2d. per bushel for grinding Wheat. The Flour is made into Bread in the Prison, and consumed by the Prisoners in the County Gaol, and by those in the House of Correction.'

(Signed) Josh Chaplin, Keeper.

Within the 1823 return, both Warwick Gaol and House of Correction had included a Schedule (B). This is the numerical breakdown of the prisoners held, types of crimes, ages, and sex covering the period of Michaelmas 1822 to 1823:

'Warwick Gaol.

Total number of Prisoners, Michaelmas 1822 = 468
Total number of Prisoners, Michaelmas 1823 = 516

Out of those the breakdown was as follows:

4/ Number of Debtors, Male = 75 – Female = 4

5/ Number of Misdemeanours, Male = 53 – Female = 9

6/ Number of Felons, Male = 325 – Female = 50

7/ Number of Prisoners Committed in the course of the Year, = 437

8/ Number of Tried Prisoners, Male = 358 – Female = 57

9/ Number of Untried Prisoners, Male = 20 – Female = 2

10/ Number of Prisoners above 17 years of Age, Male = 334 – Female = 53

11/ Number of Prisoner under 17 years of Age, Male = 44 – Female = 6.

12/ Greatest Number of Prisoners at one Time, = 190

13/ Number of Prisoners who have been Committed before;
Once, = 63
Twice, = 18
Three times, = 6
Four and more, = 0

14/ Prisoners Employed;
Hard Labour, = 38
Employment not being Hard Labour, = 21

15/ Prisoners not Employed, = 54

16/ Punishments for Offences within the Prison;
Whipping, = 6
In Irons, = 0
Solitary Confinement, = 0
Other Punishments, = 12

17/ Number of Solitary Cells, and of Apartments below Ground;
Solitary Cells, = 3
Apartments below Ground, = 0

18/ Cases of Sickness and Death;
Cases of Sickness in the Year, = 41
Greatest Number of Sick at one Time, = 18
Deaths, = 1.

House of Correction.

Total Number of Prisoners, Michaelmas 1822 = 725
Total Number of Prisoners, Michaelmas 1823 = 700

Out of those the breakdown was as follows:

4/ Number of Debtors, Male = 1 – Female = 1

5/ Number of Misdemeanours, Male = 439 – Female = 129

6/ Number of Felons, Male = 126 – Female = 6

7/ Number of Prisoners Committed in the course of the Year, = 700

8/ Number of Tried Prisoners, Male = 211 – Female = 24

9/ Number of Untried Prisoners, Male = 347 – Female = 118

10/ Number of Prisoners above 17 years of Age, Male = 504 – Female = 123

11/ Number of Prisoners under 17 years of Age, Male = 50 – Female = 23

12/ Greatest number of Prisoners at one Time, = 196

13/ Number of Prisoners who have been Committed before;
Once, = 35
Twice, = 15
Three Times, = 3
Four and more, = 1

14/ Prisoners Employed;
Hard Labour, = 63
Employment not being Hard Labour, = 50

15/ Prisoners not Employed, = 28

16/ Punishments for Offences within the Prison;
Whipping, = 64
In Irons, = 3
Solitary Confinement, = 9

17/ Number of Solitary Cells, and of Apartments below Ground;
Solitary Cells, = 4
Apartments below Ground, = 0

18/ Cases of Sickness and Death;
Cases of Sickness in the Year, = 73
Greatest Number of Sick at one Time, = 18
Deaths, = 3.'

Even though these returns may seem at first light as being fairly detailed, and seemingly transparent, we should take a step back and consider that their authenticity is only as good as the truthfulness and honesty of those who wrote it. It wouldn't have been the first or last time figures have been manipulated for one's own personal benefit!

Footnotes

1. Formerly known as Sheep Street, situated in the north of the town, it was named as such because it was the main route for sheep farmers bringing in their livestock on a Saturday into Warwick Market.
2. Back then, unlike today, bank notes were printed all over England in nearly every county, which made forgery all the easier. Sadly, most of those hanged for 'uttering' (knowingly passing on or using forged bank notes) were unknowingly passing on forged notes still in circulation at the time.
3. Going back to the aftermath of the Napoleonic Wars, Britain's coffers were empty. As such, the silver shilling was the most minted currency. This led to cottage industries rising up in such places as Birmingham, for example, where shillings would be either filed down or clipped around the edges; as all shillings were edged, edging tools were used to hide the fact that they had been filed or clipped. The shavings of silver would then be melted down, and a stamp and die used to create a

new shilling. If caught with an edging tool, clippers, stamp, or die, you would be charged with 'coining'. However, if you were caught with a shilling that had been filed down so much that it defaced the king's head, then it became 'high treason–coining' as it was seen as an attack on the Crown.

4. Henry Tattnall was somewhat of a colourful character. The son of John and Alice Tattnall, Henry was born in Warwick in 1768, where he was baptized at St Nicholas Church on 9 May the same year. After being educated locally, he became assistant to the then-gaoler, William Roe, who himself had learnt his trade from his father, also named William Roe.

   On 25 January 1795, Henry married 16-year-old Suffolk-born Eliza Cooke at the Collegiate Church of St Mary's in Warwick and settled in their living quarters in Warwick Gaol. At the time, the gaol was riddled with disease; sadly, only six years after their marriage, Eliza died at home on 30 September 1801, aged just 22.

   Two years after Eliza's death, Henry remarried to 24-year-old Kineton-born Esther Bayliss at the Collegiate Church of St Mary's Church, where he had married Eliza. The marriage didn't begin well, as after their wedding they returned to their quarters at Warwick Gaol; this was when Esther realized the true horror of her new home and fled back to her father in nearby Southam. Henry followed her and persuaded her to return. It was unknown then that Esther returning would have a dramatic effect on not only their relationship, but also on the lives of the women and children being held in Warwick Gaol and the newly built Bridewell (House of Correction) on Barrack Street.

During the following years, Esther didn't only accept her surroundings but became involved in the care of those women and children. Many of the children were the offspring of prostitutes, who had been abandoned, as they were seen as accidents of their mother's profession. Others were 'criminals', like the 10-year-old boy who had been arrested and incarcerated for stealing a lemon from a Warwick Market stall for his sick mother.

In 1806, the tables turned on Henry, when he was called before Warwick Assizes to show good cause why he shouldn't be arrested for contempt of his office after a prisoner had escaped. The very fact that Henry continued as gaoler after 1806 would indicate that he escaped punishment and kept his job.

In late 1815, Henry and Esther welcomed in their first child and son, Charles, who was baptized at the Collegiate Church of St Mary's in Warwick on 10 November.

Henry remained as gaoler until around 1826, when he retired and was succeeded by Henry Adkins. Henry left Warwick and moved to neighbouring Leamington Spa, where the family resided in Grove Street, and where in 1832 Henry died.

After Henry's death, Esther remained at Grove Street with Charles, and continued with her good works in leading the way for prison reforms for women and children.

Esther would later write a book entitled *Prison Discipline, A Narrative of Twenty-Three Years Superintendence of the Women and Boys' Wards in the Gaol at Warwick*. Edited by member of Parliament for North Warwickshire and high sheriff of Warwickshire (1819) Sir John Eardley Eardley-Wilmot, Baronet, it was first reviewed in the *London Literary Gazette* on Saturday, 9 April 1836. Esther remained at Grove Street, and was joined by her sister, Ann Bayliss, and son Charles up until her death in October 1853, aged 74.

Chapter 6

Trial & Retribution

In this chapter, we'll focus on Ann's trial and the testimony given. After seven long months incarcerated within the cold walls of Warwick Gaol, having endured horrendous conditions, during which time she had lost her newborn child, the day of Ann's trial finally arrived.

Around 10.30 am on Monday, 10 April 1820, the slight figure, dressed in a grey gown and shawl, clutching a bottle of smelling salts in one hand, appeared from the gaol steps into the packed main court room of Warwick Assizes. Ann was followed by three other felons, Joseph Pace, George Butler, and John Cooper, who were to stand trial for burglary of the house of Mr Phillips of Wilton, near Birmingham, and also of shooting at Mr Phillips with the intent of killing him.

All four were put to the bar, but it would be Ann who would face the full force of the judiciary first, standing before all six of Sarah's children as they sat sobbing. Ann was described as being no more than five feet tall, with long brown hair, brown eyes with high cheek bones, and being the possessor of some personal beauty.

Her judge that day was His Lordship, 53-year-old Somerset-born Sir William Draper Best,[1] later the first Baron Wynford, of Wynford House, Wynford Eagle, Dorset.

With the jury having been sworn in, the other three felons were dismissed and returned back downstairs to their cells until after Ann's trial. Her twelve-man jury was: Thomas Suffolk, Henry Smith, John Willson, Thomas Smith, Thomas Prickle, Thomas Hinks, John Drake, John Taylor, George Watson, Phillip Kench, Thomas Miller, and surprisingly, Kenilworth surgeon Dr William Bodington's uncle, Mr Joseph Cattell!

It wasn't unusual in England for the jury to have consisted of all men; it wouldn't be until the twentieth century when both men and women sat together on a jury during a criminal court case in England. However, the myth that it wasn't until the twentieth century that the first all-female jury first sat is just that – a myth, as we saw in the previous chapter.

The clerk of the court, Mr Henry Dalton Lowndes, read out Ann's charge of murder–petty treason. 'That on Sunday, 29 August last, she did murder her mistress, Mrs Sarah Dormer, at Dial House Farm, Ashow, and how did she plead?'

'Not guilty!' Ann replied.

And so, this charade began, as the lead solicitor for the prosecution counsel, Thomas Denman[2] of the Leigh family of Stoneleigh Abbey, let his colleague,

William Reader, open the case for the prosecution by calling to the stand all of their witnesses.

The first witness to be called was Sarah's eldest, Elizabeth Dormer. After confirming her name and her relationship to the victim, she confirmed that her siblings and the other three servants all being present were in the house that day. Elizabeth said that she remembered the prisoner being charged with taking away some notes. It was then when Sir William interfered in the proceedings and prevented Elizabeth going into evidence on this point.

Elizabeth continued by stating that they had two guests arrive that morning, and when her father returned, he had brought the two Brays with him. They all had tea together, which her mother had made, and the prisoner had waited on them.

Sir William interrupted by stopping the trial to make the announcement that the court had received intelligence that blood had been shed in Scotland in a contest between the people and the military. The incident Sir William was referring to occurred near Greenock on the last day of the week of unrest and strikes in Scotland in 1820, between 1 and 8 April, known as the Radical War or the Scottish Insurrection. This resulted from high unemployment, high food prices, and unfair working conditions following the end of the Napoleonic Wars, as well as the introduction of the 'Corn Laws', which deliberately increased the price of corn at home by increasing taxation on cheaper imported grain. The casualties on 8 April numbered eighteen, including an 8-year-old boy and a 65-year-old woman.

The unrest at the time wasn't just limited to Scotland; only thirteen days prior to Sarah's murder, another confrontation occurred at St Peter's Square in Manchester, and was to be known as The Peterloo Massacre. The youngest casualty recorded was a 2-year-old boy, who had been knocked out of his mother's arms by a drunken cavalryman as she crossed a road.

It's unclear what the motive was of Sir William interfering in Elizabeth's statement for a second time with the news from Scotland, as at the time it was two days old, and most likely to have been reported in the national newspapers.

Elizabeth continued with her evidence by stating that she, her sisters Harriet and Mary, and her brother Joseph, with William Hinde, had left Dial House around 6 pm to visit the Aldridges at Thickthorn, leaving her father, the Brays, Thomas Harris, and the prisoner alone with her mother in the house. She claimed that they had returned at 7.10 pm, and found Ann at the end of the hallway looking very agitated, and perspiring very much. Elizabeth then described the events leading up to her sister Mary discovering her mother's body, and her discovering the bloodspots on the hallway floor; she believed that someone had attempted to wipe them up. Sir William asked Elizabeth if she was quite sure they looked as if they had been wiped. 'Yes', she replied, 'they looked wiped as if smeared along.'

We can take nothing new from Elizabeth's evidence which we don't already know, except for the fact that Elizabeth stated that she had been home that day with all of her siblings, but then left with her sisters and brother Joseph to visit the Aldridges. She claimed they left her father, the Brays, Mr Thomas Harris, and Ann alone in the house with her mother; it's strange she doesn't mention her two other brothers, James Harris and John, because if they hadn't left with Elizabeth, they must have stayed at the house!

Sir William asked Ann if she had any questions for Elizabeth: 'No, my Lord.'

The next to give evidence was Sarah's youngest daughter, now aged 14, Mary.

Mary stated that she and her sisters, Elizabeth and Harriet, with her brothers, had left the house for the Aldridges. Mary continued with what we already know of her discovering her mother's body, but she didn't see any blood. Mary contradicted Elizabeth by claiming her brothers, meaning Joseph, James Harris, and John, were with them when they left the house. Sir William had asked Ann again if she had any questions for this witness, and again Ann had politely declined.

The three farm servants each took their turns in giving evidence of the times they had left the house and returned, of which we have already learnt. Next was Thomas Harris, who confirmed that he had visited the Dormers and around 6 pm he had left for the wake with the Brays and Mr Dormer, and were seen off at the front gate by Mrs Dormer. At the same time as they had left, Miss Dormer (Elizabeth) and her party had also left to visit the Aldridges, leaving Mrs Dormer and the prisoner alone in the house. Ann was again asked if she wished to question the witness, and again she declined.

11-year-old Maria Lee Dormer was called next. Sir William explained about taking the oath, and cautioned her that she must tell the truth. Maria explained she knew Mrs Dormer and that she and her little brother visited the house at 6.30 pm; she saw no one else at the house except for Mrs Dormer and the prisoner. She and her brother were given a glass of wine each and cucumbers before they left the house shortly afterwards. Ann had no questions to ask of Maria.

Elizabeth Jaggard followed Maria in giving evidence. She was at the house called the Forge on the day of the murder with Miss Russell, who lived there. She rode to Ashow and passed the house of Mr Dormer just before 7 pm. As she passed, she saw Mrs Dormer by the middle window, apparently reading with her spectacles on. At the same time, she saw a woman come out into the lane and look down it towards the direction of the village. She was dressed in a red gown, had on a coarse apron and cap, and she went away almost immediately. She believed that the woman didn't notice her. As she rode past on her way home, she had seen the same woman being taken to gaol wearing the same gown as she had seen her wearing when she had come out into the lane. Ann declined to question the witness.

Sarah's eldest son, Joseph, was next to take the stand. Joseph, under oath, stated that he and his sisters returned home from the Aldridges just after 7 pm, and upon his sister opening the door, she was very much struck by the appearance of the prisoner, who looked greatly agitated. He was standing by the court pailing when he heard screaming. He immediately ran into the house and upstairs, with the prisoner following. He took hold of the prisoner and led her out into the middle of the lane and said to her, 'You have murdered my mother.' She gave no reply. He was much enraged and pulled her along, when she said 'I will go where you choose to take me, you need not pull me.' Witnesses cannot say if he charged her with his mother's murder more than once.

Joseph's evidence is interesting. First, he confirms his sister Elizabeth's evidence when she said that she was with her brother when they had left and visited the Aldridges, but contradicts his sister Mary when she said that she had left in the company of her brothers. It's also strange and unnecessary when he repeated Elizabeth's statement upon the discovery of Ann in the hallway; that wasn't his evidence, it was hers. Considering he was around the backyard at the time, how would he have known unless he had been coached? However, the most damning is that we will see he lied under oath. Once again, the prisoner declined the offer of questioning the witness.

Of Sarah's children, only Elizabeth, Joseph, and Mary spoke. No word was heard from Harriet, James Harris, or John before they left the court room.

Henry Beesley was next up. Henry stated that he had entered the house after hearing the young girl's scream, and upon doing so found a light and traced bloodspots on the hallway floor leading to the best kitchen, where he discovered a pair of spectacles on the floor and a book on the table. Henry made no comment about the chair in which Sarah was seen next to the middle window by Miss Elizabeth Jaggard as she rode past just before 7 pm. Ann had no questions for the witness.

William (Dormer) Pope followed Henry onto the stand. William said that he was drawn to Mr Dormer's house as he was passing by and heard a girl's scream. He witnessed hearing Mr Joseph Dormer say a girl had murdered his mother, and heard the girl reply that she had not, and saw him strike her on her left cheek. 'I asked her if she had seen anyone about the house, to which she replied "No", and did you go out of the house, "Yes, to the woodpile."' William ended his statement by informing the court that the woodpile was about twenty yards from the house. Once again, Ann declined to question the witness.

Even though Henry and William were witnesses for the prosecution and therefore hostile, their evidence could have been invaluable to Ann's defence, if she hadn't been so unlawfully and cruelly denied one. Their evidence proves that Joseph Dormer lied; along with his sisters' contradictory evidence, this would have made them unreliable witnesses. It would have also brought into serious doubt Ann's so-called confession, as we will see later.

The final two witnesses to be called were Kenilworth surgeon Dr William Bodington, and Kenilworth Constable Thomas Bellerby. William read out his report of Sarah's injuries and wounds, which we already know about. Thomas read out Ann's confession, which again we know. With her confession, we have to question not its content, but the means by which it was obtained.

Ann had denied Sarah's murder twice that evening. The following morning after discovering the two bloody aprons and hand towel in the back garden, the constable claimed that he had ridden from Dial House towards Stratford-upon-Avon, where near Alveston, he claimed that he told Ann he had apprehended her brother, Thomas, for his concern in Sarah's murder, because there was only circumstantial evidence against Ann. She was discovered in the house by the children (doesn't prove that she murdered Sarah), and her hands looked bloody as if they had been wiped (again, doesn't prove she had wielded the knife). So what hypothesis was he working on to believe a second person was involved, and why did he believe that person was her brother Thomas?

At the time, Thomas Heytrey was employed as a blacksmith at Pimlico, a farm near Alveston and just north-west of Stratford-upon-Avon, which is about fifteen miles the constable would have ridden to get there from Dial House. It's strange Thomas Bellerby never said where or how he knew where he was, or the reason why he had apprehended him. Neither did he say what Thomas Heytrey had said of the accusation of his involvement in Sarah's murder.

Sir William asked Ann several questions:

William: 'Why did you not run away?'

Ann: 'I was so confused I didn't know what to do.'

William: 'What did you do after committing the crime?'

Ann: 'I came back downstairs into the kitchen.'

William: 'How long was it after the crime when the party returned?'

Ann: 'About ten minutes.'

William: 'Did you have a knife when you went into the best kitchen and knocked your mistress out of her chair?'

Ann: 'I had not.'

William: 'Had your mistress done or said anything in the course of the day to offend you?'

Ann, who had stood firm and resolute throughout the trial, finally broke down in tears. Gripping the bottle of smelling salts, she replied: 'She had not given me one angry word, I liked my mistress very much, and would have gotten up at any hour of the night to serve her.'

With the case for the prosecution having closed, Sir William turned to Ann and called upon her for her defence, and asked if she had any witnesses to call. Head bowed, Ann replied that she had none.

The learned judge turned to the jury and gave them his direction on the evidence, cautioning them to carefully weigh the facts, though it was difficult to remain unprejudiced after what had been heard.

The offence was petty treason, for the law had made a distinction in such cases to excite a horror in persons in the prisoner's station against taking the lives of those entrusted in their charge, but the committing of the offence was not to make the jury find the party guilty.

It was necessary for them to be clear that the deceased and the prisoner stood in the situation of mistress and servant in order to constitute the crime. There was not one pretence to show a provocation for the dreadful murder.

Sir William continued by going over the evidence and concluded by observing that there was abundant proof that the deceased was murdered, and murdered by the prisoner at the bar; that independent of the confession made to the constable, the deceased was in perfect health, and the wounds could not have been inflicted by her own hands.

It was highly to be lamented that the unfortunate woman retired to the very worse place she could have gone; had she fled into the open air, she might have saved her own life, and that of the prisoner. The case was one of the clearest of circumstantial evidence, it seemed nearly as much so as that mentioned by a great law authority, when a murderer is taken running away with the bloody knife in his hand. It appears that even the confession is so circumstantial in itself, it could not have been invented by the prisoner for any purpose whatever; the facts were minutely detailed by her.

The jury, after consulting together for a few minutes, brought in their verdict: 'guilty' of both petty treason and murder.

The clerk of the assizes, Mr Henry Dalton Lowndes,[3] asked Ann what she had to say and why sentence of death should not be passed on her. Ann hesitated, as if she was going to give detail of what had taken place, or didn't understand the question, and said, 'She was coming out of the dairy, and had been working all day' – and then, as if she had just realized the question and recollected herself, she answered 'Nothing!'

Sir William leant over the side of his chair, took the black cap from off the hook, placed it on his head, and began his sentencing:

'It was satisfactory in such a horrid transaction that her guilt was so fully made out, that her own confession was not necessary – that confession wrung from her conscience, was not required to substantiate the charge. Lest the Jury should feel prejudice, he had deemed it proper to stop them going into some of the evidence which was offered as to former transactions – she had no temptation to commit a horrid act. She had destroyed at the moment of the murder, the life of a benefactor, who had once saved her from punishment for a capital offence, for which her life must have been then a sacrifice – what could have induced her to the committal of so foul a crime! She had suffered her passions to run away with her, & now she might tell those around her, how dangerous it was to give them the rein.'

Sir William 'trusted her fate would warn all to attend to that religion, which could alone preserve them from crime – he could give her no hope, the next day but one she must meet her God in judgement. He would say nothing to aggravate her fate, but it must not be suffered to be held out to others, that repentance was everything; let none be sure that they ever can be saved from the effects of a dreadful crime by a repentance before they die – from the fanaticism that exists a delusion of this nature too much prevailed.

'The rest of her short time would be passed with a Reverend Clergyman, who would tell her duty, and it only remained for him to state to her, what the Law announced for persons in her situation – That on Wednesday next, she be drawn upon a hurdle to the place of execution, and there be hung until she be dead, and that her body be given to the Surgeons for dissection.'

The clerk of the assizes, Henry Dalton Lowndes: 'Do you have anything to say why your execution should be stayed?'

Ann: 'No. I have not.'

Sir William: 'Then may God have mercy on your guilty soul.'

Ann was then led out of the court room, back downstairs into the gaol, where she would spend the last hours of her young life in isolation, fed only on bread and water, and only receiving visits from the gaol chaplain, Reverend Hugh Laugharne, and the gaol staff.

That evening, it is claimed Ann wrote the first of two letters she had written, which were to be delivered to the addressees after her execution. The first was to Sarah's eldest, Elizabeth.

Dear Miss Dolmer 10 April 1820

I take the liberty of addressing you with the epistle for the last time, and I am heartly sorry for the sorrowful misfortune as has happened which I hope the lord in his mercies will forgive me and I was very sorry to see you look as bad. I did not know you when you were called up. I hope you will forgive me for what I have done as my life will pay for the unfortunate deed, oh may the almighty be your comfort and may he pardon me my sins. Miss Dolmer, I ask your forgiveness and the family's at large for I forgive all the world and I hope I shall die in charity with all men, may the almighty be merciful to me. Dear Miss Dormer it is not the distress us I have brought on myself but what I have brought of your family and my own and I hope I shall be a warning to everyone to avoid the temptations of the infernal spirit, I hope the lord will be your comfort such a good creature as I acknowledge you to be, farewell may the lord power down his blessings on you and yours. I must conclude with my prayers as it is all I can give at this time; I am your unfortunate servant. Ann Heytrey.

The second letter was written to her mother, Mary, on the eve of Ann's execution.

My Dearest Mother 11 April 1820

I take this opportunity of writing to you, I hope my dear mother you will resign your troubles to the lord, may he be your comforter, and I hope we will meet in heaven: my heart is resigned to the lord, may he have mercy on me. My Dear Mother this is the last morning of my being in this world, but I hope in God by this time tomorrow I shall be in a glorious world, where there is no fear of death or trouble. My dear and tender Mother, I once more and forever bid you farewell; my last wish is for you not to grieve for me, an unfortunate sinner, but offer your trouble up to almighty, as he will be your comforter and protector. I hope I shall be a warning to everyone, never to deviate from the laws of God, but to walk in his ways. Farewell, my dear Mother, may the lord bless you is the prayer of your unfortunate Daughter.

My Dear Mother,

I conclude with my love to Mrs Rings, and I hope she will not think of nothing that is past, I hope God will bless her and hers in this world, and that they may enjoy happiness in the next. I most heartly repent, and I forgive all the world, and I hope the world will forgive me.

Ann Heytrey

Both letters should be treated with caution of their originality, as in her first addressed to Elizabeth Dormer, she misspelled her surname twice 'Dolmer'. As for her last heart-breaking letter to her mother, Ann gives her love to a Mrs Rings, but doesn't mention her sister Hannah or brother Thomas. Which, as someone who had to write my last good-byes to my wife and family prior to the Land Battle of the 1991 Gulf War, I find it strange why she didn't mention Hannah and Thomas!

Footnotes

1. Sir William was born on 13 December 1767 at Haselbury Plucknett, Somerset, the third eldest son of Thomas Best. He was educated at Wadham College in Oxford, entering at the age of 15 in 1782. But left two years later,

having failed to achieve a degree, as he had intended to enter the church but chose law instead.

With a degree in law, William entered the Middle Temple on 9 October 1784, before being called to the bar five years later in 1789. In 1794, William married Mary Anne Knapp, who he would go on to have ten children with. In 1802, he was elected as the member of Parliament for Petersfield, East Hampshire, as a Whig, a position which he held until 1806. After switching to the Tories, he sat for Bridport, Dorset from 1812. The following year, 1813, William was appointed as the solicitor-general to George the Prince of Wales, later King George IV. He held that post until 1816, when he was appointed attorney-general to the prince. In 1818, he became the chief justice of Chester.

In 1819, William became a judge of the common pleas, and also was raised to the peerage as the first baron Wynford. At home, on 3 March 1845, he died, aged 77.

2. Thomas Denman was born in London on 23 July 1779, the son of Dr Thomas Denman. He began his education at the age of just four at the English Nonconformist Protestant Palgrave Academy, in Palgrave, Suffolk. English dissenters, Mr Rochemont (Minister) and Mrs Anna Laetitia Barbauld, who didn't conform to the Church of England, ran the academy.

   After going on to Eton, Thomas finally graduated from St John's College, Cambridge with a law degree in 1800. In 1802, he married Theodosia Anne Vevers, and in 1806, he was called to the bar at Lincoln's Inn and at once went into practise. Thomas' rise was rapid, during which time he had defended the Luddites in January 1813, and gave a brilliant defence of Queen Caroline of Brunswick in August 1820, just four months after Ann's trial.

He would go on to represent both Wareham and Nottingham as their member of Parliament. Afterwards, Thomas was appointed as the attorney-general, and was knighted within the administration of Prime Minister Lord Grey on 24 November 1830. Two years after, he was appointed as lord chief justice of the king's bench and raised to the peerage as the first baron Denman of Dovedale in the county of Derby.

On 16 February 1841, as lord high steward, Thomas presided over the earl of Cardigan's trial in the House of Lords for assault committed by duel with the intent to murder Harvey Garnett Phipps Tuckett. (Fellow 11th Hussar Captain Douglas, was the earl's second and was also on trial.)

At the time, Prince Albert had been given the rank of colonel within the 11th Hussars, and this may have been the reason why the earl and Captain Douglas were found innocent. On 26 September 1854, Thomas died at home, two years after his wife, in Stoke Albany, Northamptonshire, aged 75.

3. The ancestor of the author on his maternal grandmother's side.

Chapter 7

Return to Dial House

We have now heard all that the jury heard during Ann's trial: witness statements, the surgeon and constable reports. After only a few minutes in deliberation, the jury concluded that she was guilty beyond any doubt. Sir William Draper Best had directed the jury to ignore Ann's confession, after letting it be read out in court, because he believed there was enough evidence, however circumstantial, to prove her guilt.

But was he and the jury right in their verdict? None of Ann's confession was questioned, which leaves us with more questions than answers. So, it's time to return and question her words, and their verdict, for the first time. Let's see if we can find the truth. Follow me as we now go back to Dial House.

The time is now 6.00 pm. William Hinde and five of Sarah's six children come out into the lane from the front of the house and start to walk towards Mr Thomas Aldridge's at Thickthorn, in the direction of Kenilworth.

At the same time, Joseph Dormer, Thomas Harris, and the Brays from Coventry left the house and headed down the lane in the opposite direction towards Ashow. Sarah saw them all off, standing at the front gate.

In Elizabeth, Joseph, and Mary's statements, they contradicted each other when stating who of their brothers had left with them for Thickthorn. James Harris, Harriet, and John never gave evidence. We know that Harriet was with them, as it was her who called out to their mother just before Mary discovered her body. As for John, being the youngest, it is understandable. But James Harris is never mentioned once, because he wasn't there. Mr Thomas Harris stated that after he had left, Sarah and Ann were alone in the house, which Ann Maria Lee Dormer also confirmed.

At 6.30 pm, Ann Maria Lee Dormer and her younger brother, Joseph Lee Dormer, the birthday boy, arrived at the back door and were invited in. Both were given a glass of wine and a cucumber snack before leaving through the front door out into the lane some ten minutes later.

From 6.00 pm, when the children and their father's guests had left, until the two young children arrived at 6.30 pm, we have a thirty-minute gap without any information. This isn't that suspicious, as Ann Maria Lee Dormer had said that she saw no one else at the house apart from Sarah and Ann. We know that John Branstone had left the wake at 5.00 pm for milking and had returned at 5.30 pm. So, by 6.30 pm, the farmyard and outbuildings would have been unoccupied for an hour. The young girl may have not seen anyone else at the house, but that doesn't mean no one was in the farmyard or the outbuildings.

After the children had left, Ann said that she and Sarah went out into the garden and collected cucumbers for the family's supper upon their return. With the cucumbers having been collected, they both returned to the back kitchen, where Ann had taken them into the adjacent pantry. Sarah had walked up the hallway and into the best kitchen, where she picked up her book, sat in her chair next to the window, put her spectacles on, and began to read.

Ann said in her confession that it was while she was cutting up the cucumbers with a few onions in the pantry that she had the thought come into her mind that she must murder her mistress. Ann put the chopping knife down. She came out of the pantry into the back kitchen and changed her apron, hanging the one she had been wearing on the back of the back door.

Having changed her apron, Ann went out into the back garden and walked the twenty yards down to the woodpile, but then returned to the back of the house and walked around to the front into the middle of the lane, where she stood and looked towards the direction of the village.

We know this as Miss Elizabeth Jaggard had given evidence to witnessing such just before 7.00 pm as she rode past, and she also saw Sarah reading with her spectacles on by the middle window. Elizabeth also said that she believed that Ann hadn't noticed her.

It's staggering that Ann was never questioned over these events. Surely by just asking one question – Why did you go out into the lane? – her intent, if that was her true intent, would have at least been established. But there again, if they feared this wasn't the case, that may be the reason why she wasn't asked.

Consider the mindset needed to have inflicted such horrific wounds on Sarah. When Ann claimed a disembodied voice came to her, telling her to murder Sarah, she had been holding the chopping knife, and knew that Sarah was completely oblivious and defenceless – but she put down the knife. Ann felt the need to change her apron – why? Did it really matter which apron she had been wearing when she murdered Sarah? Or was she going to meet someone? Let's just say, for an example, where she says she did go after changing – down by the woodpile, twenty yards from the house and in the direction of Chesford Bridge.

Miss Jaggard also said that she thought that Ann hadn't noticed her. Considering that Elizabeth was on horseback, and where she must have been to have seen Sarah by the middle window, she could have only been a matter of yards from Ann as she stood in the middle of the lane.

There is no way that Ann couldn't or wouldn't have noticed her. This would indicate that Ann was unconcerned by Elizabeth's presence or, in fact, anyone approaching from that direction – the same direction she would have expected Sarah's children to be returning from. Ann also knew that Mr Joseph Dormer and his guests would be expected to be returning home from the direction in which she seemed transfixed. Was she looking and hoping to see Joseph coming home? If so, why?

After spending only a few moments in the lane, Ann hurried back to the house and back kitchen. By now, Miss Jaggard had ridden past, as Ann entered, walked up the hallway into the best kitchen at the front, went straight up to Sarah, who was still sat reading, and knocked her out of her chair onto the floor.

Ann claimed that she had stood over her for about a minute before Sarah had got to her feet and ran out of the room, into the hallway, and upstairs into her bedroom. Ann followed her into the hallway, stopping halfway to pick up the carving knife from the dairy, and then proceeded upstairs and into Sarah's bedroom, where she found Sarah lying on her back on the floor. Ann said that she thought that Sarah had either fainted or tripped on the carpet.

This at first seems quite plausible – well, it did to the jury and Sir William Draper Best, as they believed it. We know Sir William directed the jury to ignore Ann's confession, but there is one problem – and that

Photo 1. Holy Trinity Church, Arrow, where Sarah was baptized (our Warwickshire).

Photo 2. As above.

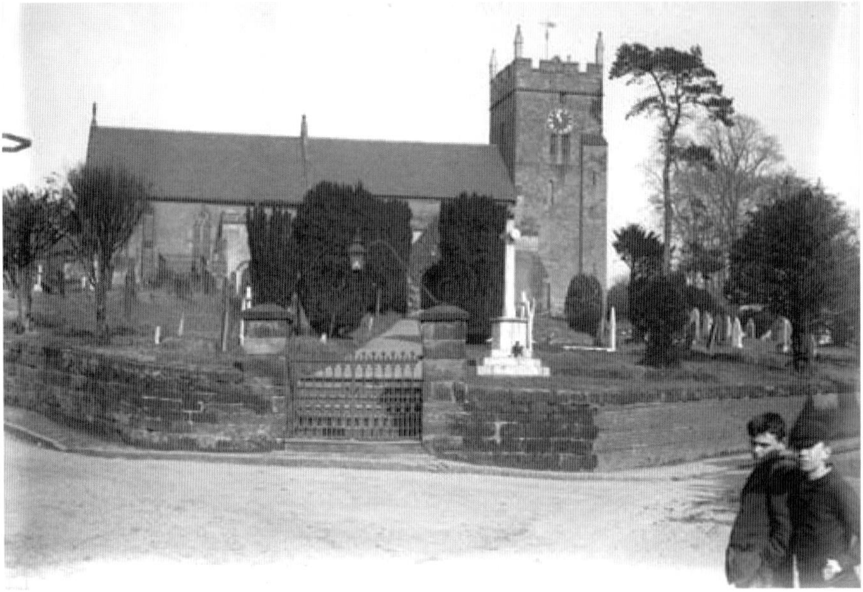

Photo 3. St Mary's Church, Cubbington, where Sarah and Joseph were married (our Warwickshire).

Photo 4. All Saint's Church, Sherbourne, where Ann's parents Mary and William were married (our Warwickshire).

Photo 5. St Leonard's Church, Charlecote, where Ann was baptized, and her parents are buried (our Warwickshire).

Photo 6. Charlecote Hall, where Ann first went into service (our Warwickshire).

Photo 7. Front view of Dial House.

Photo 8. Dial House farmyard.

Photo 9. View of the village of Ashow from the back of Dial House.

Photo 10. Thickthorn Manor, where Sarah's children had visited Mr & Mrs Aldridge on that evening. And where the author's parents first met, and where they lived in the early 1970s.

Photo 11. The view looking down the lane towards Ashow from outside of Dial House, where Ann was seen looking down just before 7.00 pm by Miss Elizabeth Jaggard.

Photo 12. Northgate Street (formerly Sheep Street), Warwick, with Warwick Assizes and Gaol entrance on the right (our Warwickshire).

Photo 13. Warwick Gaol dungeon air vent (Author's collection).

Photo 13A. Warwick Dungeon.

Photo 14. The Assumption of Our Lady Church, Ashow (Author's collection).

Photo 15. Joseph and Sarah's headstone (Author's collection).

Photo 16. Warwick Assizes courtroom where Ann was tried (Unknown).

Photo 17. Warwick Assizes Bible on which Ann would have sworn at her trial (Unknown).

Photo 18. Sir William Draper Best (First Baron Wynford) Ann's trial judge (National Portrait Gallery, London).

Photo 19. Sir Thomas Denman (First Baron Denman) painted in 1819. Prosecution council at Ann's trial (National Portrait Gallery, London).

Photo 20. Chesford Crossroads (Author's collection).

Photo 21. Opposite direction view Ann was seen looking down just before 7.00 pm, and from where Sarah's children would have returned home from (Author's collection).

Photo 22. St Nicholas Church, Kenilworth, where so many of those in this story were either, baptized, married or are buried (The Heritage Group).

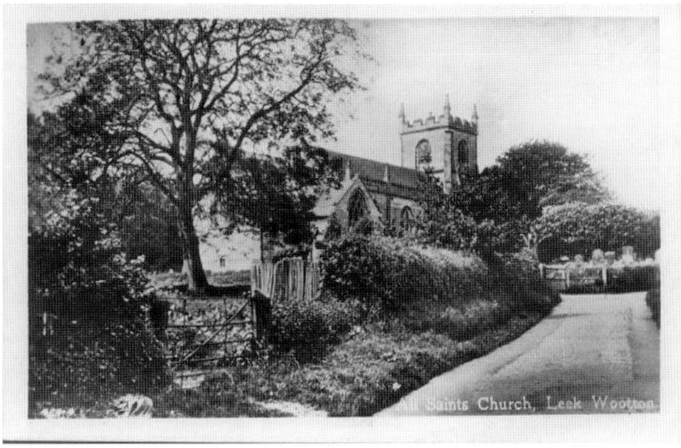

Photo 23. All Saints Church, Leek Wootton, where Maria Lee and her brother, Joseph Lee Dormer, were baptized and where their parents were married (our Warwickshire).

Photo 24. Chandos Leigh (First Baron Leigh) of Stoneleigh, who was charged with murder (National Portrait Gallery, London).

Photo 25. Stoneleigh Abbey, where there were several murders, including Sarah's, on the estate (Royal Collection Trust).

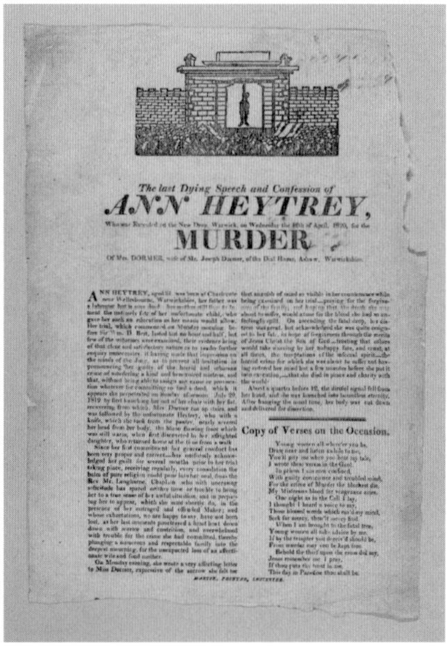

Photo 26. Penny Dreadful (Public domain. No copyright).

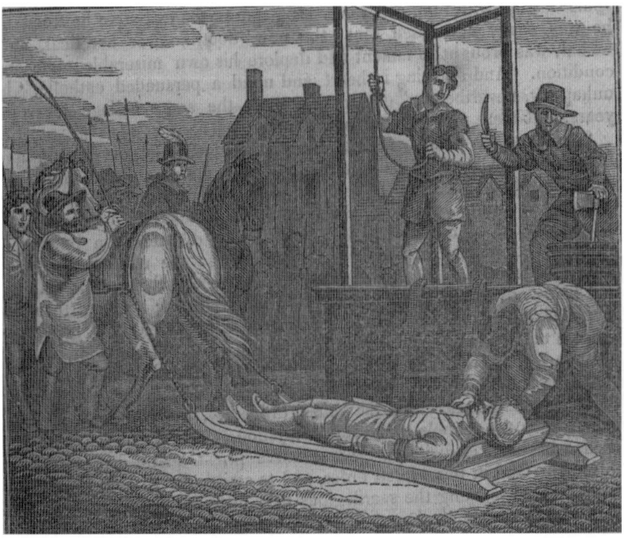

Photo 27. Hurdle (Public domain. No copyright).

Photo 28. Montague House (back) Kenilworth (Public domain. No copyright).

Photo 29. Montague House (front) Kenilworth (Public domain. No copyright).

Photo 30. Chesford Bridge (Looking down the direction Ann has been seen looking down, still looking for James).

Photo 31. Seed Drill (From the early-mid 19th century).

Photo 32. Dial House Farm (Farmyard drive entrance sign).

Photo 33. Sarah's bedroom window, showing Ann's face (An echo from the past still there).

Photo 34. Thought to be one of the original Dial House Farm signs.

Photo 35. Dial House, the top middle window is Sarah's bedroom, and when zoomed in on, I took the one of Ann's face (Photo 33).

Photo 36. Warwick Gaol entrance.

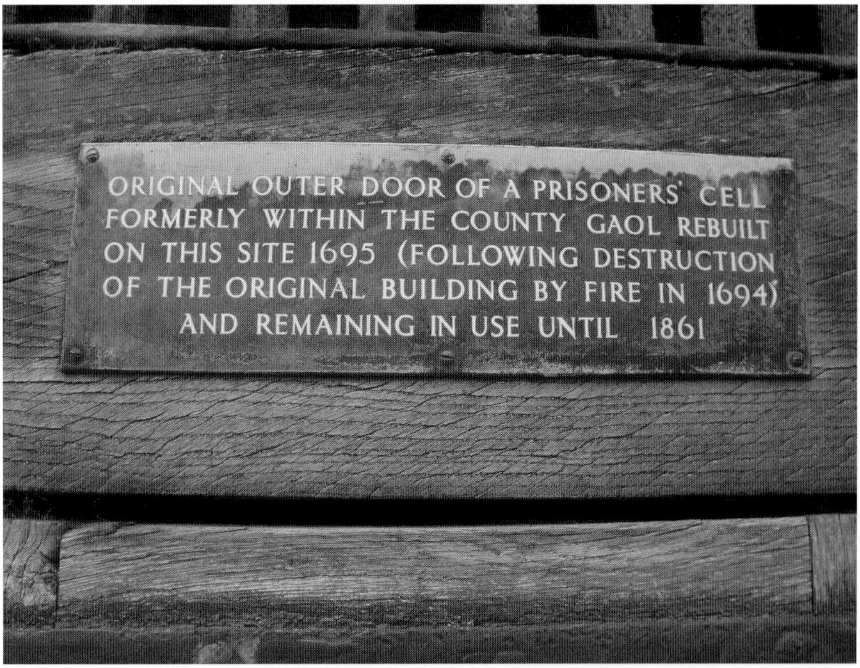

Photo 37 and 37A. Original Gaol outer cell door from the same period + sign above door.

is, once heard, her confession cannot be unheard, and it must have influenced them in their verdict.

If we go back to when Ann enters the back kitchen, she knew that the chopping knife was in the adjacent pantry, where she had been using and left it only minutes before, but she ignores it. Ann walks up the hallway towards the best kitchen – halfway along, she passes the dairy, ignoring the carving knife that she later claims she had taken before following Sarah into her bedroom. Sir William did ask Ann if, when she knocked Sarah out of her chair, she had the knife in her hand. She had said that she had not!

Ann had walked up to Sarah, knocking her out of her chair onto the floor. If this is true, Sarah was sat by the window in full view of anyone passing, which apparently Ann was completely unconcerned about being seen doing, and again brings into question her reason for going out into the lane.

Sarah, as we are led to believe, was sat reading as she was knocked onto the floor. Again, if this was true, why then did Henry Beesley find a pair of spectacles on the floor, but her book on the table? Sarah must have stood up and put the book on the table, and then been attacked, which contradicts Ann's claim, and why would Sarah have needed to stand up when Ann came in? It's very unlikely that Ann had surprised her to the extent that she would have needed to stand up, as the one person in the world who Sarah would have expected in the house was Ann!

Ann had stood over Sarah for about a minute, watching her on the floor, before Sarah had got up and was allowed to run out into the hallway. Why did Ann just watch as Sarah was on the floor, vulnerable? But there again, as Ann was unarmed, she couldn't have killed her then. Was this interaction planned so as to get Sarah out of the room, with the hope that she would run upstairs and into her bedroom, where Ann could kill her without being seen? Wasn't Ann taking a chance that when in the hallway, Sarah could run out of either the front or back doors? As Ann was behind her, she couldn't have stopped Sarah from doing so.

Sir William alluded to this during his sentencing of Ann, when he said that if the victim had run into the open air, she may have saved her own life and that of the prisoner. Why didn't Sarah get out of the house when she had the opportunity to do so? Had Ann locked both doors before attacking her, and then afterwards unlocked them? We know that when the children returned, they found the front door shut but not locked.

We already know from Elizabeth Dormer and Henry Beesley's statements that blood spots were found on the hallway floor, which Henry traced to the best kitchen, and Elizabeth believed someone had attempted to wipe them up, as they looked smeared. Ann couldn't explain the spots when Elizabeth asked upon discovering them.

There is no doubt that the blood was Sarah's. She came from the best kitchen after the attack into the hallway, and she was bleeding – but from where, and what had caused it?

Ann was unarmed when she attacked Sarah. So, we can exclude all of Sarah's wounds, as they were inflicted upstairs in her bedroom, from where she never left. That leaves just her injuries.

If we refer back to Kenilworth surgeon Dr William Bodington's report, he states that Sarah had several small scratches on the left side of her face, and a violent bruise on her nose. One of her front teeth was knocked out from her upper jaw, also another from her lower jaw opposite the former, and several bruises appeared on various areas of her body.

We can eliminate the bruising on her body and the small scratches as sources of the blood, which leaves us with two of her teeth having been knocked out, and her violently bruised (broken) nose.

Firstly, her two teeth: Henry Beesley never mentioned finding two of Sarah's teeth by her spectacles in the best kitchen. In fact, there is no mention if they were found, indicating that she may have swallowed them while lying on her back during the knife attack upstairs in her bedroom. This may also explain why only teeth opposite each other were knocked out – most likely by the knife.

As for her violently bruised (broken) nose, this logically seems to be the cause of the blood spots. Ann did say that she had 'knocked' Sarah out of her chair; she must have used her fist to break Sarah's nose before she fell onto the floor. But this doesn't explain why, if at the time, Sarah had been holding her book, why the book was found on the table.

This also begs a further question. If Ann had punched Sarah in the face and broke her nose, and maybe even knocked two of her teeth out, when Constable Thomas Bellerby examined Ann's hands more than an hour after the event, why did he only find dried blood on them and under her nails? He makes no mention of seeing any bruising, swelling, cuts, or grazing on her hands, which if there had been, he would clearly have said. The conclusion we can take from this is that whoever broke Sarah's nose, it couldn't have been Ann!

We should also look at the blood spots themselves. It would be only natural for Sarah, having received a broken nose, to have run down the hallway with a hand over her nose. The blood would have run down onto her mouth, which she would have also covered with the hand, and therefore it would be unlikely that she would have left as many spots on the floor. This would indicate something else.

Ann found Sarah lying on her back on her bedroom floor. She had then leant over Sarah and began cutting her with the carving knife. Sarah gave little or no resistance, until she had cut her two or three times. Sarah didn't speak but gave a rustling sound and caught at the knife with her hands. Ann then held Sarah down until she was dead, and replaced the white cap back on her head, which had come off during the struggle.

Ann then lifted Sarah's arm and placed the knife under it by her side, with the intention of making others believe that Sarah had done it herself, before picking up the piece of flannel and wiping her hands on it. She threw it down and forgot about it before leaving the room and closing the door behind her.

All Sarah had to do was to get into her room, close and lock the door, open her window, and call for help, but she didn't. It's strange: when Mary screamed out after discovering her mother's body, all of those outside, including in the farmyard, heard her. But no one heard Sarah cry out – or maybe she wasn't able to!

We need again to refer to Dr William Bodington's report. Ann claimed that she had cut Sarah two or three times, and that Sarah had put up little or no resistance. In William's report, Sarah had two deep cuts to her left jaw, and her spine had been cut more than once. Her two teeth were knocked out, and the defensive cuts on her hands would suggest she deflected other cuts. So this wasn't as Ann had claimed – everything points to a frenzied attack.

Ann said that after cutting Sarah two or three times, she held Sarah down until she was dead. This again doesn't bear scrutiny, as William said the first cut which divided all parts of her spine would have been fatal, severing the carotid arteries, the jugular veins, and spinal cord, resulting in complete paralysis below the wound, and extreme blood loss.

What happened after Ann had closed Sarah's door and returned to the back kitchen is confusing, to say the very least. To piece together the sequence of the events that followed Ann leaving Sarah's bedroom, we need to first ignore her confession, as it ended when she returned to the back kitchen.

We need to go back to the blood-stained flannel found under one of Sarah's shoulders, and the hand towel and two aprons Constable Bellerby discovered in the back garden, as well as the answers Ann gave when she was questioned about these items.

Ann had held Sarah down until she died. She then put Sarah's white cap back on her head, which Ann had claimed had come off during the struggle – but Sarah gave little or no resistance, which is a contradiction. Also, why did Ann put the cap on Sarah's head? Could this not be seen as a sign of respect, and even endearment?

Ann said she picked up the piece of flannel, wiped her hands on it, then threw it down and forgot about it.

Yet this piece of flannel was found under Sarah's body – if Ann had thrown it down after Sarah's death, how did it get under Sarah's body?

Then Ann comes out of Sarah's room and closes the door behind her. We know Sarah's door was closed from Elizabeth Dormer, who said that when she passed the room, she noticed that her mother's door was closed. Ann turns around and takes the hand towel from off the banister and wipes her hands on it, taking it with her as she returned downstairs to the back kitchen.

When Sir William questioned how long it was, after returning to the back kitchen, before any of the party returned home, Ann had claimed about ten minutes. Considering Sarah was last seen alive just before 7.00 pm, and Elizabeth Dormer walked in and found Ann at the end of the hallway at 7.10 pm, it was impossible for her to have committed the murder and have waited in the kitchen for five minutes before Elizabeth came in, never mind the ten minutes claimed.

Ann came into the back kitchen with the blood-stained hand towel and the blood-stained apron she was wearing. Constable Bellerby questioned Ann about the blood-stained hand towel and apron he discovered hidden underneath other towels soaking in the large tub by the back gate. Ann had said she had put them there. Though he had asked where she took the hand towel from, he never asked how blood came to be upon the apron, nor was this ever established. It must have been presumed it was the one she had been wearing during the murder!

Ann must have changed her apron, maybe into the one she had changed out of earlier and had hung on the back door. She goes outside into the back garden and submerges her hands into the soapy water in the tub, putting both the towel and apron underneath the other towels soaking. She then returned into the back kitchen just in time as Elizabeth enters and finds her by the back door, which is quite plausible, but cutting it fine. Ann's reason for putting both in to soak was that she was planning to wash them out the following morning, after just murdering Sarah, who still lay bleeding on her bedroom floor – completely implausible.

However, we still have to explain the blood-stained apron found rolled up on the floor of the shed by the back door – where did that come from? Ann was not asked how it got there, but was asked how blood came to be upon it. She answered that she couldn't tell. Which is strange, as she claimed she had committed the murder, and no one had helped her. She could therefore have been the only one who put it there, and must have known how blood had come upon it, but the young woman couldn't tell. Or was the truth that she didn't know?

Let's go forwards to 8.30 pm, when Constable Thomas Bellerby arrives at the house and finds Ann stood at the front gate with Samuel Turner. Thomas said that he had examined her hands which had dried blood on them and under her nails, and her hands looked as if they had been wiped. He also said the apron she was then wearing was free from blood. We can presume that apron was the one she had changed into after taking off her blood-soaked one.

There is one more question which needs asking, which has been nagging like a toothache, and that is: Why, over an hour after the murder, did Ann have blood on her hands and under her nails, and why was the apron she was wearing then was free from blood?

If we go back to when Ann wiped her hands on the piece of flannel, it must have been covered in Sarah's blood. Ann leaves the room and shuts the door. Later, Mary opened that door by the handle that Ann had used only minutes before, but Mary never mentioned any blood on her hand after opening it.

Ann then takes the hand towel from off the banister and wipes her hands for a second time on it a few seconds after. She returns to the back kitchen and changes out of her blood-soaked apron, her hands still bloody. But no blood was transferred onto the apron she had changed into. She goes out into the back garden and submerges her hands in soapy water to hide the hand towel and apron underneath the other towels. Is it possible after wiping them twice and submerging them in water only a few minutes after murdering Sarah, her hands would still have blood on them, and the apron she had changed into with bloody hands could be free from blood over an hour later?

When Elizabeth entered the house at 7.10 pm, she had found Ann at the end of the hallway by the open back door. Ann looked to her very much agitated and was perspiring very much. She had asked Ann if anyone had been in the house since they had left. 'No, nobody' was her reply – which was untrue, as the two young children, Ann Maria Lee Dormer and her brother, Joseph Lee Dormer, were there at 6.30 pm.

Sir William had asked Ann why she didn't run away after the murder. She had replied that she was so confused that she didn't know what to do, which is quite understandable. Regardless if Ann was guilty or not, where could she have run to? There was only her sick mother back home in Charlecote, which would have been the first place the authorities would have looked for her. And if she was innocent, why run? The fact would have been used against her, because why run if she had no reason to do so? If she had accomplices, she would surely have left with them. She was left in between the proverbial rock and a hard place, and let's not forget the elephant in the room – that she was at least two months pregnant at the time!

It was then that Elizabeth said that Ann had gone out into the back garden and down to the woodpile, which as we know from William (Dormer) Pope's statement was about twenty yards from the house. William had also asked Ann if she had seen anyone about the house; again, the reply was to the negative. He also asked if she had been out of the house, which she confirmed as doing to go to the woodpile. Ann had gone to the woodpile twice, a fact that she didn't hide. What was so important about the woodpile for her to visit it twice within an hour? On both occasions, she wasn't collecting wood for the fires!

Elizabeth claimed that it was during Ann's short absence that she noticed blood spots on the hallway floor. She believed they looked smeared as if someone had attempted to wipe them up, thus alluding to Ann having tried to cover them up. Upon Ann's return, Elizabeth pointed out the blood spots and had asked Ann what she had been doing. According to Elizabeth, Ann had replied, 'Oh nothing'. Elizabeth also claimed that Ann still looked agitated and very much confused.

Ann had been sent to fetch a mop and clean up the blood spots. Upon her return, both sisters, Harriet and Mary, claimed that they had asked Ann where their mother was, and claimed that they received different replies: that Sarah had gone out towards the village, and that she had gone into the garden ten minutes ago to collect cucumbers. Considering Ann's confusion, it is possible she had reverted to her own recent memory in replying, as she did go out into the garden to collect cucumbers, and did also go out into the lane to look down towards the village.

It was after, when Harriet had called out to her mother and received no reply, that Elizabeth went upstairs with Mary following her. Elizabeth said that as she passed her mother's door on the landing whilst heading towards her own room, she had noticed that her mother's door was closed. As Elizabeth entered her own room, Mary had opened her mother's door and saw her lying on her back, her heels towards the door, but didn't see any blood, then screamed out 'Murder, my mother is murdered'.

Sarah's eldest son, Joseph, was stood by the court pailing when he heard his youngest sister scream. Joseph ran into a barn, picked up a pitchfork, and ran into the house and upstairs into his mother's room with Ann following him. He grabbed Ann by the arm and dragged her out of the house and into the lane, where he accused her of his mother's murder in full view of all who were passing.

We know that Joseph claimed that Ann had given no reply, but we also know that Joseph lied from William (Dormer) Pope's statement that he had witnessed this, and heard Ann reply that she hadn't!

We also should question Joseph's motive for dragging Ann out into the lane in full view of everyone who were either stood by or passing the house before he accused her of his mother's murder. Surely, he had the opportunity upstairs on the landing outside of Sarah's room as Ann had followed him upstairs, but he chose to drag her outside where, in full view, he accused her.

As for Elizabeth, when she first entered the house and saw the state Ann was in, it is interesting that she never asked if Ann was OK or whether she was ill. In fact, she showed no concern at all, but only asked if anyone had been in the house since they had left – but what at that time made her believe that anyone had? Ann had said that no one had, which we now know, and she knew, was untrue, as the two young children had been there at 6.30 pm.

Ann had left the house and had gone down to the woodpile before returning almost immediately. It was during her short absence that Elizabeth said she had noticed blood spots on the hallway floor. Elizabeth had asked Ann what she had been doing, presumably referring to the blood spots, to which Ann had replied, 'Oh nothing'. Elizabeth was insistent that the blood spots looked smeared, as if someone had attempted to wipe them up, implying that it was Ann who had done so, and as such, she had known they were there and how they came about.

Elizabeth was the first to give evidence in court, and mentioned Ann's previous charge of taking the bank notes. Sir William was correct in interrupting her, as Ann was standing trial for Sarah's murder and not the previous charge.

We know that Sarah's children had left to visit Thomas Aldridge at Thickthorn, along with William Hinde. Elizabeth, Joseph, and Mary all contradicted each other regarding how many of the siblings went, as John and James Harris were never mentioned by name. Nor did they, Harriet, or William Hinde give witness.

The truth is that there is no proof that John and James Harris actually went there, as we don't know what time they arrived or what time they had left. Thomas Aldridge was never asked, nor were they!

If the children had left the house at 6.00 pm, it would have taken them around twenty minutes to have walked to Thickthorn, arriving at around 6.20 pm. The entrance to Thickthorn was further north on the Leamington Road (A452) by 400 yards than it is today. For them to have returned to the house by 7.10 pm, they would have had to have left by 6.50 pm.

Given all that we now know, the court testimony given doesn't make much sense of the events of that fateful evening, as it is full of questions and contradictions. Ann's own confession is contradictory to the evidence. By going over the discrepancies, a possible hypothesis of what really could have happened is brought to light, which we will explore in the next chapter.

Chapter 8

Hypothesis

This chapter contains this author's supposition or proposed explanation, made on the basis of limited evidence as a starting point for further investigation.

Before we begin, we need to remember that at the time of Sarah's murder, Ann was at least two months pregnant. The child's father was Sarah's second eldest son, 20-year-old James Harris Dormer. Upon the discovery of Ann being pregnant, and James being the father, 'the guilty party' was sent into exile with his cousin, James Lee Dormer, and his family in nearby Leek Wootton.

There can be little doubt that discovering Ann was expecting James' child came as a great shock to Sarah and Joseph – thus the reason why the charge against Ann for taking the bank notes was made to disappear. As her child would be their first grandchild, he or she, along with the mother, needed to be protected.

Sarah and Joseph needed breathing space to arrange for the future. So, James was sent away. He couldn't be sent to family in Ashow, as it was too near, and tongues would surely start to wag, as questions of why he was there would be asked. So, he would be sent to Leek Wootton with his cousin, where he would be accepted without question or suspicion.

However, Ann would be looked after, at least until she gave birth. We will never know what plans Sarah and Joseph had – whether they would have allowed Ann and James to have married, or if Ann was to have returned home to Charlecote after the child's birth, with the Dormers looking after and bringing the child up.

Ann wouldn't have been able to leave the farm, and James wouldn't have been able to return home without the permission of his parents.

But Ann and James had an ally in 11-year-old Ann Maria Lee Dormer, unknown to Sarah and Joseph, and maybe even Ann Maria's own father, James Lee Dormer. In the court report, Ann Maria was recorded as intelligent for her age, which was slightly patronising, but no doubt true.

We can now begin to unravel the events of that evening. It's 6.30 pm when Ann Maria Lee Dormer and her brother, Joseph Lee Dormer, knock on the back door of Dial House and are invited in. We know the reason why 9-year-old Joseph went to see his great-aunt, Sarah: it was his birthday. However, as for Ann Maria, not only was she chaperoning her brother, but she had a written or verbal message from James for

Ann to arrange a meeting time and place by the nearby Chesford Bridge near the woodpile.

Leek Wootton is situated not far from the northern bank of the River Avon. It wouldn't have taken much for James to have walked down the hill to one of the boathouses, take a boat, and row the short distance downriver to the Chesford Bridge and the nearby woodpile.

Ann Maria Lee Dormer said that they had left the house via the front door, after seeing no one else in the house apart from Sarah and Ann. We can only speculate as to the time they had left, but let's say it was around 6.40 pm. Ann claimed that it was shortly after the children had left when she and Sarah went out into the garden to collect cucumbers for the family's supper.

Having collected the cucumbers, both women returned to the house and back kitchen. Ann had taken the cucumbers into the adjacent pantry, where she began to chop them up with a few onions. Meanwhile, Sarah walked up the hallway into the best kitchen at the front of the house, sat in her chair by the middle window, put her spectacles on, and began to read from her book.

It was at this point Ann claimed that she had heard a disembodied voice in her head telling her she must murder her mistress. This is extremely doubtful, and very convenient for her to have heard it then.

Ann had finished preparing supper, and with Sarah at the front of the house, she took the opportunity to go down to the woodpile, conceivably where James may have been planning to meet her. Ann put down the chopping knife, came out of the pantry into the back kitchen, and changed her apron, wanting to look presentable for James.

Ann goes out the back door and heads down the garden in the direction of Chesford Bridge to the woodpile, but she never made it there. Two or three people, who she didn't recognize, were loitering in the farmyard and caught her attention. She was concerned, or even in fear of their presence and possible intentions. It was this fear that either she, Sarah, or both could be in danger which forced Ann out into the middle of the lane, hoping that she would see Joseph Dormer returning from the direction of the village.

This would explain why Miss Elizabeth Jaggard had thought that Ann hadn't noticed her. Ann couldn't have been unaware of the young woman riding towards her, but Ann knew that she wouldn't have been able to help – or worse, could have even put her life in danger. Likewise, Ann knew and would have expected William Hinde and Sarah's children to be returning from Thickthorn from the same direction as Miss Jaggard was approaching from, but wasn't concerned to look. In fact, Ann seemed to have been unconcerned about anyone near her.

Not seeing Joseph Dormer returning, Ann rushes to the back of the house and enters through the back door as Miss Jaggard rides past the house and down the lane towards the village.

If we accept that it is very doubtful that Ann was Sarah's murderer, whoever did commit the murder wouldn't have come just on the off chance that the two women would be alone. They wouldn't have gone there either without prior knowledge of the family, house, and farm, which would indicate that whoever killed Sarah must have been local. But how would they have known that Sarah and Ann were alone?

This also excludes the theory that Ann's brother, Thomas, was involved, as Ann didn't know that she and Sarah would be alone until 6.00 pm. How would Ann have contacted her brother to tell him?

We know that by 5.30 pm, when John Branston had returned to the wake after milking, no one outside of the family could have known of their plans at 6 pm. Granted, the two young children arrived at 6.30 pm and left around 6.45 pm; whether anyone knew who they were and had stopped to ask them when they left isn't worth consideration. This leaves us with only two possibilities within the family themselves.

William Hinde and the children had walked towards Kenilworth to visit Mr Aldridge at Thickthorn. Apart from the family and Mr Aldridge, no one else would have had prior knowledge of the visit. So, what's the chance of them encountering someone coming the opposite direction who would have asked if Sarah and Ann were alone? If anyone had, unless they were known to the family, I would doubt that they would have told them.

We are only left with Joseph Dormer and his party, who also left the house at the same time as William Hinde and the children. It's safe to assume that Joseph and his party had ridden down to the wake, as it's very unlikely that the Brays would have walked the eight miles that morning from St Michael's Coventry to Ashow, and then walked back later that evening; they may have been slightly worse for wear by then in that case.

It's no more than a fifteen-minute ride from Dial House to the village, so Joseph would have arrived at the wake around 6.15 pm. As we know, the three farm servants were there. If someone who knew the three farm servants by sight, and was known to Joseph and was held in his confidence, had welcomed Joseph upon his arrival, and asked one simple question – whether Sarah and the children would be joining him – that person would have discovered that Sarah and Ann were alone.

This information could have been used by the questioner or passed on to a third party, who had at least thirty minutes to get to the house and commit Sarah's murder in complete confidence that the two women were alone – because there was no other way of finding out!

Ann rushed into the back kitchen from the lane as Miss Jaggard rode past the house. Ann found those who she had seen moments earlier in the farmyard now in the house. As they entered the best kitchen, Sarah, having been taken by surprise, had stood up, putting her book on the table as she faced her assailants.

Ann was kept away from the door, her view partially blocked, as Sarah was struck in the face, her nose broken. As she fell to the floor, her spectacles landed next to her.

Henry Beesley had discovered Sarah's spectacles on the floor and her book on the table, which is important evidence, as is what he never mentioned. The very fact that he didn't mention her chair means that he saw nothing untoward about it, as it must have still been upright, completely contradicting Ann's confession that she had knocked Sarah out of her chair while she was reading, book in hand.

Sarah lay dazed for a minute on the floor before she was picked up by two of her assailants, as the third still held Ann at bay. Sarah was dragged under her arms along the hallway, her head bowed with her chin resting on her chest, and blood dripping onto the floor. This would explain why Sarah hadn't tried to leave the house – she wasn't able to. It also explains the bruising on other areas of her body, as she was manhandled along the hallway. This would also make the blood spots look smeared, as if they had been walked on, as Elizabeth Dormer believed.

As Sarah was being dragged along the hallway and upstairs, the third of Sarah's assailants, who had been holding Ann at bay, had gone down the three stone steps and into the dairy, grabbing the carving knife before following the other two into Sarah's bedroom, with Ann following on behind.

If we pause for a second and go back to the morning after the murder, Constable Bellerby visited Ann in Warwick Gaol and informed her that he had apprehended her brother, Thomas, for his involvement in Sarah's murder. Ann's reply is interesting as she had replied that neither her brother nor no other man had to do with the murder.

Why didn't she just say no one else - why no other man? Surely this implies that they may have been all females involved, and who else could have worked there to have known where the dairy was, and that a carving knife was kept there, and who else would have known which room was Sarah's bedroom? Unfortunately, no record has been found of who Sarah's maid was before Ann, or the reason why Sarah needed to employ Ann as another.

Sarah was thrown down on her bedroom floor as the carving knife was passed to one of the two assailants now in her room with her. One was brandishing the knife while the other struggled with Sarah's hands, trying to keep them away from the knife. It is clear from Sarah's defensive wounds that the poor woman had struggled, trying to protect herself from the blows until the bitter end. This also contradicts Ann's confession that Sarah had given little or no resistance.

With Sarah having taken her final breath, the two assailants in her room fled, one of whom had taken the hand towel from off the banister as she fled downstairs and out into the garden, where she took off her own blood-soaked apron, putting both her apron and the hand towel at the bottom of the tub.

The second had run downstairs into the back kitchen, and as they left, had taken Ann's old apron from off the back door, wiped their hands on it, and discarded it in the shed as they also fled out into the garden and made their escape. They were followed by the third, who just ran out, leaving Ann on the landing looking into Sarah's room in complete shock, confusion, and disbelief, and no doubt traumatized.

Ann went into Sarah's room and was confronted with the horrific scene of her mistress almost decapitated; she leant over her, picking up her white cap and replacing it on her head in a sign of respect. This was when blood had transferred onto her hands. Ann came out of Sarah's room, closing the door behind her, and went back downstairs into the back kitchen – maybe checking that Sarah's assailants had left. As she had stood by the back door, Elizabeth Dormer had returned and found her standing there, still very much confused.

Ann had gone out into the back garden and down to the woodpile. Was she making sure Sarah's assailants had truly left the farm, or was she looking for and hoping to see James for help? But he wasn't there, and she would never see him again. Even recently, she has been witnessed still looking for him.

Ann's confession ended at the point when she returned to the back kitchen. When asked by Sir William what she did after committing the crime, she stated that she had returned to the kitchen. She gave no mention of going out into the garden before Elizabeth Dormer had returned at 7.10 pm, and therefore was completely oblivious to what happened outside with the blood-stained hand towel and aprons. This would mean that Ann wasn't guilty of Sarah's murder, and that the apron she was wearing when Miss Jaggard saw her in the lane just before 7.00 pm was the very same one she had been wearing at 8.30 pm when Constable Bellerby arrived at the house and commentated on it as being free from blood.

If it wasn't Ann, who was it, and what was their motive?

Chapter 9

Possible Motives for Murder

'There is a reason for everything, and everything has a reason!'

Another mystery with this case is that no motive was ever established apart from the voice Ann had claimed had come to her instructing her to murder her mistress: we can now exclude that with confidence, because Ann didn't kill Sarah. But someone did. What could have been the reason why a 59-year-old farmer's wife and mother of six was targeted, beaten, and brutally slain within the four walls of her own home? No money, property, papers, or livestock were recorded as being stolen, so we can exclude burglary. Neither was there any damage or arson recorded.

Sarah was the target, beyond any doubt, as they had left Ann unharmed. The reason was probably that Ann hadn't been in Sarah's employment for longer than five months, so she wouldn't have had much opportunity to have visited the village and less so to have known its residents.

Confident that Ann couldn't have identified them, they left her to take the blame – you could even say that they left her carrying the baby, which we know she actually was. Leaving Ann unharmed could also be seen as vengeance in their minds for her escaping the hangman when she was caught with the bank notes in her possession. They may have believed that if it had been one of them, they would have surely been hanged.

Before we explore any possible motives, we should examine Sarah's murder. Its method by knife was face to face, and deeply personal to the assailant, showing extreme violence. That the murder was committed in her own home indicates control and violation over the victim. It shows signs of extreme hatred and utter contempt and indifference for Sarah and her surroundings, and complete disregard of the possibility and consequence of being caught in the act. Whoever murdered Sarah had some serious mental issues and a history of violence from a young age, which must have come to the forefront and had been recognized locally before Sarah's murder!

Motive 1: The Outsiders

We need to go back to Sarah and Joseph's marriage at St Mary's Parish Church, Cubbington on Monday, 6 July 1795 by special licence. Remember, there is no record of any of Joseph's close family being present, but their two witnesses were Sarah's father, John Harris, and Joseph's uncle, John Judd.

We also know about the cost and trouble of marrying by special licence. Of the three main advantages of doing so, one sticks in mind, and that is that the wedding banns would be circumvented, allowing the union to be consecrated in secret. No prior warning would be given of the forthcoming marriage in either the groom's or bride's parishes. Considering the Assumption of Our Lady Church in Ashow, Joseph's home village, was fully operational, this would indicate that their marriage wasn't or wouldn't have been blessed by Joseph's family, or maybe by the village.

But what reason could Joseph have had to feel the need to marry in secret, spiting his family in doing so? Had his parents, who were both born locally, arranged a marriage with a local farmer's daughter as they began their local empire-building? Maybe Joseph had rejected the arranged marriage after falling in love with a young girl in Cubbington. If so, what would be the fallout, not only within his family, but also within his betrothed's family and the local community generally? It would be known that he had chosen an outsider over one of their own, going against his family's wishes!

It is believed that Joseph and Sarah may have spent their first few months of married life with Sarah's father before setting up home in Stoneleigh. This is speculation, as no record to confirm this has been found. However, as the children came along, all were baptized at the Assumption of Our Lady Church in Ashow, which may indicate that Joseph and Sarah's union may have been accepted by Joseph's close family for the sake of the children, and Sarah accepted into the fold.

But this doesn't mean that the village had accepted her. At the time of the baptisms, St Mary the Virgin Church in Stoneleigh had been allowed to fall into a state of total disrepair by the Leigh family of Stoneleigh Abbey, so this may have been the only reason why the children were baptized in Ashow.

It is believed that Joseph and Sarah had taken over the tenancy of Dial House Farm around 1814 or 1815, after the Adkin family had left. Again, we can only speculate as to what had gone on during the interim years. Not meaning to speak ill of the dead, we don't know anything about Sarah's character. Nor do we know if, within the village, the resentment towards her had grown; now she would be seen as the lady of the manor sitting upon high and looking down on, and over, them.

There is very little doubt that when moving into Dial House Farm, Sarah would have employed at least one maid as the children were growing up. Who they were is unknown, as is the reason why by 1819, Sarah needed to employ another (Ann).

We can only speculate as to the reason why the maid Sarah had employed had left the vacancy for Ann to fill. The Dormers would have been expected to have employed locals whenever possible, supporting the local economy, as times were hard. This begs the question why Sarah employed another outsider like herself in Ann and not a local girl.

Let's just say, playing devil's advocate, that Sarah's previous maid was a local girl, and that the relationship between Sarah and the villagers had completely broken down to the point that she never trusted her maid not to have been telling tales to the village about her, her house, and her family. This could have been the reason that Sarah dismissed her. Thus, Sarah would be seen as denying a local family of an income, and Sarah could have then employed Ann, who had no links or any allegiances to the villagers. If true, how would this have been taken in the village?

Sarah employed Ann in March 1819, and if there was any resentment between her and the village before, this would have driven a wedge even further into their relationship and isolated her from the village. Was this the reason why Sarah employed another outsider – someone she could trust? Unknown to Ann was that she had just walked into a perfect storm, the aftermath of which would tragically cost her own life and that of her child's, over something she was completely unaware of and never saw coming.

We know that in June and July 1819, only a few months after Ann's employment, she had discovered that she was pregnant with Sarah's second-eldest son's, James Harris Dormer's, child. Fearing that when the family found out, she would be thrown out with nowhere to go but back to her ill mother with another hungry mouth to feed, Ann takes bank notes from the Dormers as insurance, for which she was charged with the capital offence of stealing in a dwelling house, for which her life would have been forfeited.

There may have been some in the village who, upon hearing the news, would have been pleased. Those who resented Sarah might have considered this as her comeuppance for employing another outsider. There is no doubt that they would have also been aware of the consequences of such a charge – that Ann would surely be hanged. Just imagine the reaction of those when the following morning she is seen in the back garden doing the washing as if nothing had ever happened. Could this have been the tipping point when resentment turned into murder?

This is, of course, speculation, as there is no proof of these events having taken place. However, if we apply an open mind and lateral thinking, it is quite compelling as an explanation for a possible motive for Sarah's murder, as is the next.

Motive 2: Christopher Leigh's Missing Monument Mystery

'Sacred in the memory of the Honourable Christopher Leigh fourth son of the Right Honourable Thomas Lord Leigh, and Lady Mary his wife. He married Penelope Cotton, daughter of Sir G. Cotton, Bart, of Cumbermere Abbey, Cheshire, by whom he had issue, Mary, Catherine, Roger, and Ferdinand. He married secondly Constance Clent, daughter of John Clent, Esqr. of the Borough of Warwick, by whom he had issue Thomas.

Roger Leigh of Haigh Hall, eldest son of the above Honourable Christopher Leigh, he married Margaret Higham, eldest daughter of James Higham Esqr. of Wigan, Lancashire, by whom he had issue, Robert and James.

> CHRISTOPHER LEIGH, OBIIT (Died) SEPTEMBER XVI (16), MDCLXXII (1673). AETAT (Aged), XLVI (46).'

Joseph Dormer was a tenant farmer of the Leigh family, of Stoneleigh Abbey, Stoneleigh, some two miles north-east of Dial House Farm. Until the publication of *The Missing Monument Murders* in 2016 by Australian author Judy Stove, nothing was publicly known of the events on the Stoneleigh Estate which occurred between

1814 and 1823, placing Sarah's murder slap-bang in the middle.

In 1154, King Henry II granted land within the ancient Forest of Arden (Shakespeare's Greenwood) to Cistercians from the Staffordshire area, who built Stoneleigh Abbey. Cistercians were an order of Catholic monks and nuns. The order had two other abbeys in Warwickshire: Merevale Abbey (1148) near Atherstone, North Warwickshire, and Coombe Abbey (1150) near Coventry. It is recorded that on Maundy Thursdays the monks of Coombe Abbey would distribute money, ten quarters of rye bread, three quarters of malt beer, and three hundred herrings to the poor at the front gate each year.

Around 1285, the monks of Coombe Abbey built Chesford Bridge near Dial House Farm; however, it is believed that there had been an earlier wooden bridge crossing the river Avon at or near that point prior to 1285.

After the dissolution of the monasteries by King Henry VIII following his fallout with the pope, all three Warwickshire abbeys were closed, and Stoneleigh Abbey Estate was purchased by Sir Thomas Leigh, then Lord Mayor of London, in 1558.

During the English Civil War (1642–1652), Coventry was a Parliamentary stronghold where Oliver Cromwell sent Royalist prisoners who were held within the city walls at St John's Church on Fleet Street, including Scottish Royalist prisoners in 1648. During their morning exercises outside of St John's Church, the local population took great delight in taunting, name calling, and throwing stones at the prisoners. It is also believed that this was when the term 'being sent to Coventry' first originated.

At this time, Christopher Leigh (1626–1672), who had inherited Stoneleigh Abbey, was a loyal supporter of King Charles I and had given the king hospitality at Stoneleigh after he had arrived at Coventry and found the gates firmly locked, when Charles headed south to London following the Battle of Edgehill. For loyalty, Christopher was given the barony of Stoneleigh.

The Leigh family would hold onto the barony until after the death of the fifth Lord Leigh, Edward Leigh, in 1786. Prior to his death, Edward had been certified as being insane after naming his two sisters, Mary Leigh and Anne Hackett, as his two 'male' heirs. It would be his sister Mary who inherited Stoneleigh Abbey after her brother's death.

It is believed that around the time of Mary Leigh inheriting Stoneleigh Abbey, a monument commemorating Christopher Leigh disappeared from Stoneleigh Church. It is alleged that the monument named his first wife and children, including his son Roger Leigh, his possible heir.

Mary Leigh died at Stoneleigh in 1806, which led to an inheritance feeding frenzy and served as the catalyst to murder. The estate passed on to the then-72-year-old Reverend Thomas Leigh, who came to Stoneleigh with his first cousin, Cassandra Leigh Austen, and her two daughters, Cassandra and the English author Jane Austen. Another claimant was Cassandra Leigh Austen's brother, James Leigh Parrot, and his wife, Jane Leigh Parrot.

Miss Jane Austen, her mother, and her sister left Stoneleigh empty-handed. Little did they know then what would follow, and maybe they were lucky to have done so.

Jane never forgot Stoneleigh and its influence on her; many references were made in her novels, including 'Mansfield Park', until her untimely death in 1817.

At the same time, Stoneleigh Church had been allowed to fall into a sad state of repair, closing it down. Considering that Christopher's monument had been squirreled away, this was slightly convenient to say the very least, and may have been a deliberate way of covering up its disappearance. Reverend Thomas Leigh brought in Richard Darley as his estate manager and architect around 1812 to breathe life back into Stoneleigh Church. As we know, he had boarded at Dial House Farm with Mr and Mrs Adkins.

Reverend Thomas died in 1813 and the estate passed to his nephew, James Henry Leigh, his wife, Julia-Judith Twisleton Leigh and their son, Chandos Leigh. It was then that a black cloud descended over the Stoneleigh Estate as Julia-Judith took over the running of Stoneleigh. Her husband had more pressing involvements away from Stoneleigh, including being the Member of Parliament for Winchester from 1802 to 1822, spending most of his time in London, residing in Portman Square, where he held several leaseholds.

Julia-Judith had full control over Stoneleigh. With her only son, Chandos, the eldest of five children, under her influence, she ruled with a bloody fist over the two square miles of the estate, which included Ashow and Dial House Farm. By then, Sarah and Joseph had taken over the tenancy of Dial House Farm, being believed to have moved from Stoneleigh.

James Henry Leigh vacated his seat as MP for Winchester in November 1822, and retired from public life under the advice of the second marquess of Buckingham, the father-in-law of his daughter, Caroline, in early 1823 and returned to Stoneleigh.

James's retirement was short lived; it was claimed that he had been discovered dead in his bed at Stoneleigh Abbey in October 1823.

We need to go back to 1814, when several suspicious deaths occurred on the Stoneleigh Estate. Two rivers flow through the estate, the Avon and Stowe. At the time, improvements were in progress on the bridge over the Stowe, designed by the Scottish architect John Rennie the elder. Of all of John's achievements, Waterloo Bridge in London must have been one of his finest, which was officially opened on 18 June 1817 on the second anniversary of the Battle of Waterloo, in honour of which the bridge was named.

One of the first believed to have been murdered was Joseph Billinge(s), one of the stonemasons working on Stowe Bridge in 1814. Joseph's death was followed by those of three other stonemasons that year: William Forbes, Thomas Proud, and Joseph Smith.

In 1815, William Blissett, a labourer on Stowe Bridge, was shot to death. Mr Daniel Dingley followed, and then John Sprawson, a Stoneleigh village carrier who was alleged to have assisted in the removal of Christopher Leigh's monument from Stoneleigh Church. John was also alleged to have been involved in the removal of the murdered stonemasons' bodies from Stoneleigh to James Henry Leigh's home at Adlestrop in Gloustershire by the order of James' wife, Julia-Judith Twistleton Leigh.

The next alleged murder was of John Leigh (II), who was a claimant to the inheritance of Stoneleigh Abbey in 1823, the same year that James Henry Leigh had died in bed. However, Julia-Judith was accused of faking her husband's funeral. James's valet, Samuel Kirkland, was accused of taking part in the murder of John Leigh (II) and in helping to fake the death of James.

There were several other witnesses to the deaths of the stonemasons in 1814, of those in 1815, and of the faking of James Henry Leigh's death and funeral in 1823, which implicated both Julia-Judith Leigh and her son, Chandos. One was Sarah (Silk) Smallbone, cook at Stoneleigh Abbey, who gave witness that under the orders of Julia-Judith Leigh, she had participated in the poisonings of the stonemasons, and in the faking of James Henry Leigh's funeral.

Sarah wasn't alone in coming forward with evidence condemning Julia-Judith Leigh for her involvement in covering up Christopher's missing monument and in the murders. Stonemason George Shaw claimed that he had been paid for taking Christopher's monument from Stoneleigh Church, and had taken part in the stonemasons' murders on Stowe Bridge.

Other witnesses were Ann (Whitmore) Perks and her husband, local plumber and gas engineer John Perks, who both remembered seeing Christopher's monument in Stoneleigh Church during their marriage in 1806. This was confirmed by John Perk's brother and witness at their marriage, Richard Perks. Also, Ann Barford, still maid at Stoneleigh, witnessed the destruction of family records on the order of Julia-Judith Leigh.

Mrs Julia-Judith Twistleton Leigh was born in 1772, and married James Henry Leigh on 8 December 1786, aged 14; she was the mother of Chandos, Caroline, Eliza, Mary, and Augusta Elizabeth. She died at Stoneleigh Abbey on 8 February 1843. Though she was accused of several murders and with faking her husband's funeral, and her son was charged with the murders of the stonemasons of Stowe Bridge, Joseph Billinge(s), and William Forbes in 1848, nothing came of it, as the State always protects its own!

Chandos became the first Lord Leigh upon his father's, James Henry Leigh's, death in 1823, and married Margarette Willis in 1819. Margarette, born on 6 April 1798, would have ten children before her death at Stoneleigh Abbey on 5 February 1860: William Henry, Edward Charles, James Wentworth, Julia Anna Eliza, Emma Margarette, Caroline, Augusta, Mary, Louisa Georgina, and Sophia.

There are several questions which need to be answered. Firstly, if Mr and Mrs Perks were married at Stoneleigh Church in 1806, it couldn't have been left in disrepair as it was the year when Reverend Thomas Leigh had inherited Stoneleigh Abbey. If it was during Mary Leigh's reign that the church had been allowed to fall into disrepair, this contradicts the reason why Thomas had brought in Richard Darley. Therefore, it would be logical that the church was closed after the Reverend Thomas' death in 1813, during which Christopher's monument had been removed when Julia-Judith Leigh's reign began.

Secondly, there seems to be enough evidence that Julia-Judith Leigh had attempted to cover up the information recorded on Christopher's monument as to his rightful heirs to Stoneleigh Abbey. So why were the stonemasons working on Stowe Bridge targeted and murdered, as the monument in Stoneleigh Church would have nothing to do with the bridge works, and what have these events to do with Sarah and Joseph Dormer?

Put yourself in Julia-Judith's position. Her husband is away and you know that your only son would inherit Stoneleigh Abbey after his father's death. You become aware of a monument in Stoneleigh Church on which another claimant to the heir is recorded. Surely, you would want to get rid of that monument. What better way of making it disappear than to hide it within the foundation of a structure which is being worked on so it would never be found – such as Stowe Bridge?

You pay off the stonemasons working on the bridge to incorporate the monument within the bridge, and then pay others to ensure their silence – but, by the evidence, this doesn't go to plan, as we have heard from witnesses who implicated Julia-Judith Leigh in the murder of the stonemasons. The question remains: how were Sarah and Joseph possibly involved, if at all, in the murderous events over Christopher's missing monument?

As Sarah and Joseph had set up home in Stoneleigh, they would have been in the middle of the events which led up to Christopher's monument going missing, and had taken over the estate flagship farm the year the murders began. Had Sarah and Joseph known something about the monument and received Dial House Farm as a sweetener to keep silent?

Another intriguing thought is that Joseph Dormer's sister, Anna Maria Dormer, gave birth to James Lee Dormer in 1788, then aged 22. James was baptized at the Assumption of Our Lady Church in Ashow on 2 March that year. On James' baptism record, Anna didn't register his father's name, which wasn't that unusual then, but she gave her son a middle name. Back then, the second-eldest son was given a second name – his mother's maiden name – as with Sarah and Joseph giving James Harris Dormer Sarah's maiden name of Harris.

Anna's name was obviously Dormer, so why give her son James the middle name of Lee? And anyway, he wasn't her second son, but her first. The name Lee doesn't appear within the Dormer family. Was this Anna's way of giving a nod and a wink to who his father was? Whatever the reason, the name Lee was important enough for James to pass it on to all his children, regardless of their birth and sex. But there again, Lee can also be spelt as Lea, or even Leigh. Now, there's a thought! Was James Lee Dormer closer to the Stoneleigh Estate than first believed? Let's face it, even back then, the lord of the manor still had unwritten special privileges!

As we already know, another incident that showed the strength of the connection between the Dormers and the Leigh family happened around June and July 1819, when Ann was caught with bank notes from the house in her possession. Joseph had ridden to Warwick Assizes to charge her, and after his return, he discovered that Ann was expecting his and Sarah's first grandchild. We know that the charge was made to disappear and no further action was taken against Ann for what was a capital offence – but how was it made to vanish so that she away with it?

It's very doubtful that Joseph had ridden back to the assizes and claimed that he had made a mistake, as they would have taken a false claim as seriously as they did the offence itself, plus his reputation would have suffered. There was one way, and that was to go to his landlord and ask for help. It was the influence the Leighs had within the assizes, with a little help from their solicitor, Thomas Denman, that covered up the charge and the reason for it being forgotten, which became apparent during Ann's later trial.

But why would the Leighs care? The Dormers were just some of many tenants on the estate, and who would have condoned such help. At the time Chandos Leigh was 28 years old. He was born on 27 June 1791, and educated in part at Harrow, where he became good friends with Lord George Gordon Byron. Chandos had a reputation as an author and minor poet. He had dined with Lord Byron in April 1816 on the evening before Lord Byron left England for Europe, never to return. It was believed this was due to his mounting debts and a scandal over his obsession with Lady Augusta Leigh.

In 1819, James Henry Leigh was still very much involved in politics and still the MP for Winchester, which kept him away from Stoneleigh most of the year, leaving the running of the estate to his wife, so we can believe that it was her who sanctioned helping the Dormers – but at what cost? At least Joseph Dormer would have slept peacefully in his bed knowing that the work on Stowe Bridge had been completed!

Motive 3: The Corn Laws and Social Unrest

In 1819, there was both social and political unrest, some of which derived from the introduction of the Corn Laws. Four years before, Britain had lost the American War of Independence, which was costly to the nation's coffers. This was made even worse by the cost of the Napoleonic Wars, which ended at the Battle of Waterloo on 18 June 1815, and caused an acute economic slump, alongside chronic unemployment and high infant mortality. The failed harvest that year and the introduction of the Corn Laws on 23 March were the catalyst for a perfect storm of civil unrest over the proceeding decades.

It wasn't just the introduction of the Corn Laws – there are many accounts of civil unrest long before 1815 throughout Britain. For example, at Birmingham in 1795, a riot broke out in response to a mill being converted to steam power, during which a young woman, Margaret Boulker had been caught throwing a stone through a window. For the crime of Rioting, Margaret was convicted at Warwick and hanged on Friday 14 August that year.

The Corn Laws imposed tariffs and other restrictions on the import of cheaper food stuffs, such as corn, wheat, oats, and barley, to ensure that prices were kept high in favour of domestic local producers. This raised the cost of bread and other food and drink to the majority for the benefit of the profits for the political power of the landowners, such as at Stoneleigh. At the time, only males could vote, and out of them, only eleven per cent were able to vote, which resulted in even more unrest as calls for political reforms grew louder.

As poverty grew throughout the nation, it wasn't just individuals who turned to crime out of desperation, trying to make ends meet, but whole families. One such local family you might recall from Chapter 5 was composed of 57-year-old, Coventry-born, Birmingham resident, Ann (Morris) Bamford, her husband, Benjamin, and children, Benjamin, William, Elizabeth, and Rebecca. Between 1816 and 1818, the family had been involved in uttering forged Bank of England notes.

Ann's husband, Benjamin, had been caught at Birmingham in 1816, and after being convicted at

Warwick had served six months in Warwick Gaol, but shortly after his release he died at home.

In March 1817, Ann's children Benjamin, Elizabeth, and Rebecca had also been caught. All three were tried at Warwick, with Benjamin being released and his sisters sentenced to death, but after a plea to the Bank of England, their sentences were commuted and they were transported to Australia for life. The following year Ann's other son, William, was caught and sentenced to death, but like his sisters, his sentence was commuted to transportation for life.

On 3 April 1818, the same day as her two daughters boarded the convict ship *Lord Wellington*, Ann was caught herself and tried at Warwick. To quash the myth that the first all-female jury first sat in the twentieth century, Ann's jury was all female: Elizabeth Hobbis (fore-matron), Mary Hobbis, Martha Pickett, Susannah Claridge, Eliza Jordan, Theresa Franklin, Sarah Price, Mary Squires, Ann Betts, Mary Canning, Maria Hobbis, and Martha Godfrey.

Ann was found guilty and sentenced to death by his Lordship William Garrow, initially dated for Saturday, 18 April, but was deferred after his Lordship had sent in a petition for mercy on Ann's behalf to the Bank of England's Solicitors, Freshfields of London. Unlike her three children, it was refused, and Ann was hanged at Warwick on Friday, 24 April alongside 22-year-old William Gray for the same crime. Ann's body was sent back home to Birmingham, where she was buried on Tuesday, 28 April at St Peter and St Paul Churchyard in Aston.

Another event which occurred in 1819, just thirteen days prior to Sarah's murder, has gone down in English history as the bloodiest political event of the nineteenth century on English soil. On Monday, 16 August 1819, some 60,000 people had gathered at St Peter's Field in Manchester to listen to members of the Manchester Patriotic Union, including Henry Hunt, as they called for radical political reforms and the ending of the Corn Laws and other social injustices.

The meeting began quietly as speaker after speaker addressed the gathered crowd. It was when the local magistrates overlooking the crowd panicked and – fearing for their own safety, which was completely unwarranted – called in the Manchester and Salford yeomanry, commanded by Major Thomas Trafford, to arrest Henry Hunt. Ironically, the yeomanry were manned by the very same landowners and mill owners who the grievances were directed towards.

The yeomanry charged down Cooper Street into St Peter's Field, and as the rearmost trooper tried to catch up with his comrades, he ran into Ann Fildes as she was crossing the road holding her two-year-old son, William. He was thrown out of his mother's arms and died instantly when his head smashed against the cobbles. William was the first casualty of what would later be named as the 'Peterloo Massacre', but not the last.

Henry Hunt was arrested and during the ensuing confusion the Cheshire Magistrates' chairman, William Hulton, called in the 15th Hussars, who four years earlier had charged Napoleon's Army at Waterloo. They drew their sabres and charged into the crowd, killing fifteen men and women and wounding between 400 and 700.

As the normally expected cover-up began, one of its victims was the *Manchester Observer*, which was closed down. The government's immediate reaction was to introduce and pass the 'Six Acts' which were aimed at suppressing any meetings for the purpose of radical reform. Thus, the self-serving Crown and State were closing ranks and protecting themselves against the very people who they were obliged to have been serving, by legislating poverty as a criminal offence. The illusion known as democracy was still far away in the distance, but at least the seeds had been sown!

The news of the Peterloo Massacre spread throughout England and gained support in its opposition in London and other national newspapers, and by word of mouth. There can be no doubt that it had reached Ashow by 29 August 1819. Early that morning, we know that Joseph Dormer had left Dial House to meet up with the two Brays (maltsters) of

Coventry, family friends and business associates. But what were 'maltsters', why were they in the area that morning, and why or what was Joseph's business involvement in them being in the area?

In the *Oxford Dictionary*, a 'maltster' is a person whose occupation is making malt, for the purpose of brewing or distilling beer. Malt is produced from the germination of either wheat or barley, but mostly barley for beer. In Britain, a Malt Tax was introduced 1697. At the time, the price was 6d per bushel. By 1819, it had increased to 2s 7d, mainly due to having to pay for the Napoleonic Wars and of course the Corn Laws. So, barley was expensive on the open market. The cheaper option was for a 'maltster' to procure it directly from the source, like a local farm for instance, but they would need a contact or middleman within that community.

Joseph and the Brays returned to Dial House at 2.00 pm, so they were out all morning and into the early afternoon. Was Joseph the middleman? Had he been supplying the Brays with barley, having changed his crop? Was this his business connection with them? It is conceivable that Joseph was introducing the Brays to local farms with the intention of signing up farmers to supply the Brays with barley at a cheaper rate than was on the open market. This would have worked in favour of both, as the Brays would get cheaper barley, and the farmers a guaranteed buyer for their crop.

For a farmer to have done this, he would have had to change his crop. To increase or introduce barley, another crop would have had to have been reduced. As barley was germinated during the winter months, would they have had to cut their wheat crop? If so, what effect would that have on the local community? Ashow had its own mill, taking advantage of the river Avon. Let's just say, for instance, that all the local farmers took their wheat to the mill to be ground into flour, and the local community bought the flour from the mill to make bread at home to feed their families.

One day, you go to the mill and you discover that the price of flour has doubled because there is less wheat being grown locally because Joseph and the other local farmers have changed their crop to barley, and it became known that Joseph was behind this. Would you see him as profiteering from your and your family's misery? Would there be suspicion that this happened because Sarah was an outsider?

This is purely speculation, as we are void of any real motive for Sarah's murder, so every possibility should be considered, however short of proof or evidence – as she was murdered, there has to have been a reason. These are three possible motives, but there could be a fourth, unknown motive, one we will never uncover, which even today is hidden within the conspiracy of silence.

About Ann's Motive

After reviewing the facts and evidence known about the case, it seems clear that Ann didn't kill Sarah. Why then did she say she did? Ann had denied her involvement in Sarah's murder twice that evening. The first was when Joseph Dormer had dragged her out into the lane and accused her of his mother's death, which she was heard denying; and the second, when Constable Bellerby arrived around 8.30 pm. It was when Bellerby informed Ann that he had apprehended her brother, Thomas, for his concern in Sarah's murder that she then gave her so-called confession.

In Bellerby's statement at Ann's trial, he never gave any reason why he believed that Thomas Heytrey was concerned, and never mentioned where he had apprehended him, or what Thomas had said in reply to the accusation. There was nothing to imply Ann was guilty, never mind her brother, who lived some 15 miles away.

It's clear that Bellerby, not getting a confession from Ann, weaponized her love for her brother as a bluff hoping she would confess to protect him – nothing less than entrapment. Once said, she could never fall back from it. What greater love could be shown for a brother than to sacrifice her life, and her unborn child's life? It's tragic that, almost a year after Ann's execution, Thomas would betray his sister's love and sacrifice, and follow her onto the same gallows!

Chapter 10

Execution

After seven long and torturous months incarcerated within the cold and dark walls of Warwick Gaol, the final morning solemnly arrived. It is impossible to imagine the night before and what thoughts had danced in Ann's mind. Those who had passed, the child she had lost, those that may have been, and no doubt of those she had now been called to face.

Ann would have been woken, if it had been possible for her to have slept through the freezing night, by Gaoler Henry Tatnall bringing in her breakfast, which normally would have been bread and water. On this morning, Wednesday, 12 April 1820, he had brought in beer instead of water for fortification, as it was to be the final morning of Ann's being in this world.

Unknown to Ann was that outside in the courtyard, preparations had begun in earnest as a team of two horses were being harnessed to the 'New Drop' gallows in its shed.

The 'New Drop' gallows were introduced around 1780. Its first victims were nine men and one woman at Newgate on 9 December 1783 for various crimes.

The gallows were wheeled. It was a large box structure with two uprights supporting two parallel beams from which a maximum of a dozen criminals could be hanged at once.

The prisoners stood on a platform, some 10 feet long by 8 feet wide over trap doors. The trap doors were controlled by a pin/bolt mechanism under the gallows, which was hidden by a black cloth drape skirting around the structure. The pin/bolt was removed by the executioner's assistant, hidden under the structure; the trap door opened; and the poor unfortunate would drop down to knee height.

Around 11.30 am, Ann's cell door was unlocked by her gaoler, Henry Tatnall, as he entered and unlocked her chains and led her outside into the cold, damp, partially lit passageway. Here the gaol priest, 66-year-old Lancashire-born Reverend Hugh Laugharne, awaited her. Ann followed him into the chapel, where she attended the Divine Service and received the Holy Sacrament, giving notice to those on the other side who awaited her imminent arrival.

The gallows had been drawn outside of the gaol and positioned at its entrance on Northgate Street. The crowd gathered – some reports say they numbered 10,000 – to witness her sad demise. Unknown to them, they would witness the last woman to be hanged at Warwick, who was innocent of any crime other than being born into a cruel world which she and those like her, who were born into poverty, could never escape, and which Ann now longed to leave!

From the chapel, Ann was led through the courts, and as she slowly walked by, she was greeted by her fellow prisoners until she reached the 'Dead Room', where Ann spent several minutes in devotion before her wrists were pinioned at her front. Outside, another horse had been brought out into the courtyard harnessed to a hurdle, which awaited her.

Just before midday, the 'dead room' back door was opened, looking out into the courtyard. As it opened, she walked out into the April daylight. She turned her head away from the burning brightness for a second until her brown eyes became accustomed to the light. She was taken out and laid on her back upon the hurdle, and then dragged the short distance outside to the gaol entrance and the gallows, and the waiting crowd stood in silence.

Ann was pulled up onto her feet and was stood before the gallows. Then the silence was broken by the tolling of the bell from the Collegiate Church of St Mary's at the end of Northgate Street as it echoed throughout central Warwick, giving notice of a young innocent life about to be extinguished, and hopefully heard by St Peter, so he could open the gates!

Henry Tatnall led Ann up the four or five steps of the gallows onto the platform, where he positioned her over the trap door with the Reverend Laugharne following her. Underneath, his assistant was hidden by the drape, ready to pull the pin/bolt.

There is no record found of who Ann's executioner was, but at the time, the gaolers were responsible for the cost of each execution, so it can reasonably be accepted that it was Henry Tatnall. In the times prior to Ann's execution, the executioner would redeem the cost by cutting up and selling sections of the execution rope to the public, which is believed to have been the origin of the saying 'Money for old rope'. This was stopped before 1820.

Before 1820, most ropes were produced locally to each county, and therefore there was no set standard of quality. There is recorded, on several occasions, that the poor unfortunate was hanged and the rope broke, leading to the prisoners being hanged more than once until the desired effect was achieved. The government introduced a set standard by introducing what was known as 'government ropes', which were all manufactured in London and had to be accounted for, thus stopping the selling of ropes.

To reimburse the cost to the executioner, the government introduced what was known as the 'tap', which allowed gaolers to produce and sell their own beer/ale within gaols. This in fact had two benefits: firstly, the gaoler would be recompensated, and secondly, the health of prisoners increased, as at the time most diseases in gaols were caused by the unhealthy water supply.

While Ann stood over the trap door, there were those mingling within the gathered crowed selling 'penny dreadfuls' (broadsides). One such being sold there, printed by Thomas Martin of Martin's Printers of Leicester, was *The Last Dying Speech and Confession of Ann Heytrey, Murder*, which was sold for a penny, and was written and published before Ann's execution. This beggars the question: how can someone claim to have heard her last words when this was written before she spoke them? Never mind that within, it records Sarah's murder on 29 July rather than 29 August 1819. Unfortunately, this nonsense has been taken as proof that Ann was guilty!

Ann's cap was removed, and the noose put over her head and tightened around her neck. A white cloth hood was placed over her head and pulled down over her brown eyes, blinding her, but with the sound of the bell still tolling for her ringing in her ears. The reverend asked her for the final time her motive for committing such a horrid crime. Ann replied: 'That I have none, but the thought I must murder my mistress; I have strong belief that God Almighty will forgive me, I truly repent of the horrid crime I had committed, and of the sins of my life. I wish Mr Dormer and his family, health and happiness, and that all those gathered would take warning of my fate.'

With her final words spoken, a white handkerchief was placed in her trembling hand for her to give the final fateful signal. Just before midday, Ann dropped the handkerchief, Henry stamped his foot down, his assistant pulled the pin/bolt, and the trap door opened, sending Ann into the darkness – into the world she had longed for without trouble, pain, and suffering. The bell no longer tolled for her.

After about fifteen to twenty minutes, Ann's body was brought back into the 'Dead Room', where she was confirmed as being dead and handed over to Kenilworth surgeon Dr William Bodington and Kineton surgeon Dr Welchman. Her body was loaded onto the back of a cart and driven to nearby Kenilworth and Dr Bodington's home at Montague House on Upper Rosemary Hill, where she was dissected in his back garden that evening.

Part of Ann's punishment was that after her dissection, her remains weren't allowed to be buried in consecrated ground. The author was sadly unsuccessful in tracing Dr Bodington's descendants, hoping to find his diary to give a clue as to where Ann's remains were buried.

Chapter 11

Echoes from the Past

We now know the full story of the tragic events at Dial House that evening of Sunday, 29 August 1819, and the brutal murder of Sarah Dormer in her own home, with no apparent motive found or given apart from Ann's own confession that she had done it, driven by a disembodied voice that had come into her mind saying that she must murder her mistress.

However, let's not forget that the real victim of the murderer was Mrs Sarah Dormer. Ann was the victim of a cruel, corrupt, and a vengeful Crown and State which twisted justice in its favour to protect itself against its greatest fear, the very people it was supposed to have defended and protected. This twisted justice even extended after death, as Ann was denied a Christian burial.

Ann was murdered, as much as Sarah was, upon the gallows in public as a warning to those witnessing this act of what will happen if they, the people, were to question or even challenge the authority of those who ruled. Those rulers feared revolution more than anything else, which was subdued with the weapon of poverty and capital punishment.

It's been over two centuries since the events at Dial House, but there are still even today the echoes and ghosts of its past in plain view, even though it is subjective. In the late nineteenth century, George Morley wrote in his book, *Shakespeare's Greenwood*, of nearby Chesford Bridge:

'On the road from Leamington to Kenilworth, there is a bridge over the river known as Chesford Bridge, originally built in the thirteenth century by the Abbots of Coomb Abbey. Clumps of woodland of a rather tangled and uncanny aspect flank the western side of the bridge, and, as might be expected of such a spot, it has long had its familiar spirit.

The figure of a woman is stated to have been seen crossing the road from the Dial House Farm, on the right of the highway to the dark woodlet on the left, where it immediately vanished. Dwellers in the scattered cottages of the neighbourhood fight shy of Chesford Bridge after dark, and although many of them have doubtless never seen the apparition which is said to "walk", the story has obtained such possession of their minds that they hold an unslayable belief in it.

I may here mention that in the year 1820 [1819] a very sensational tragedy took place at the Dial House Farm; a woman named Ann Hawtrey [Heytrey], employed probably as a domestic there, having a barbarous manner had taken the life of her mistress, Mrs Dormer, whose descendants still occupy the house. The unhappy murderess is described as being the possessor of some personal beauty, but this did not save her from the gallows, for she was hanged at Warwick on 20 April [12 April] of that year, in the presence of ten thousand people.

Probably the appearance of the "White Lady" of Chesford Bridge may be traced to the above gruesome fact, for it is notorious that scenes of deeds of bloodshed in the minds living in or near the spot invariably become haunted, either by the spirit of the murderer or by that of the murdered person, and in this case it may be that the spirit of the miserable woman, in remorse for her crime, visits the scenes of her former abode, and in the glimpses of the moon moans and sighs round the house and then disappears in the darkness of the adjacent thicket.'

Even though George's account is very informative, he does make two errors in dates, as we know that Sarah was murdered in 1819, and not in 1820, and Ann was hanged on 12 April, not on 20 April. His last paragraph sounds more like it was written by Charles Dickens in his *Christmas Carol* than it does with any reality. However, there is some substance in what he wrote. During this author's research, I had traced and contacted the daughter of one of the past owners of Dial House, and was given details of two events that happened when she was growing up there.

On the first occasion, the family were sitting in the living room watching TV. It was a still evening just before Christmas, when both the front and back doors simultaneously flew open and slammed shut. The only way both doors could be opened was if the door handles had been pushed downwards – was this Sarah showing her anger of not being able to escape the house?

The second occasion was in her mother's bedroom, which just happened to have been Sarah's bedroom and where she was murdered. Early one morning, her mother's door flew open, and an apparition of a woman ran in, screaming, before disappearing. Could this have been Sarah, again venting her anger at not being able to run up into her room, where all she had to do was to lock her door, open her window and call for help out into the lane? (But there again, why didn't she just run out of the house?)

This author was also informed of two other recent sightings at the house. The first was seeing a young woman dressed in period clothes come running from the front of the house out into the lane, then down towards the village of Ashow, followed by a young man, also in period clothes, a minute later, with a concerned expression on his face. Could it have been Harriet Dormer running down towards the 'wake' to tell her father, Joseph, of her mother's murder? As for the young man, could it have William Hinde? I always wondered how Joseph was informed of his wife's death.

The second sighting came shortly after the first on another visit to Dial House. A full-bodied apparition of a young woman was seen leaving the house, down towards the back garden, down to the Chesford Bridge. Once there, she looked over the eastern wall down towards the direction of Leek Wootton before she vanished. Was this Ann, and is she still looking for and hoping to see James?

We have now come to the end of this tragic story. I ask you, dear reader: do you believe Ann was guilty or innocent? What say you?